MAR   2012

Japan

Japan

BY BARBARA A. SOMERVILL

Enchantment of the World™
Second Series

Children's Press®

An Imprint of Scholastic Inc.

NEW YORK   TORONTO   LONDON   AUCKLAND   SYDNEY
MEXICO CITY   NEW DELHI   HONG KONG
DANBURY, CONNECTICUT

Frontispiece: Mount Fuji

Consultant: Robert Pekkanen, Chair of the Japan Studies Program,
University of Washington, Seattle

Please note: All statistics are as up-to-date as possible at the time of publication.

Book production by The Design Lab

Library of Congress Cataloging-in-Publication Data

Somervill, Barbara A.
  Japan/by Barbara A. Somervill.
      p. cm.—(Enchantment of the world. Second series)
  Includes bibliographical references and index.
  ISBN-13: 978-0-531-25354-0 (lib. bdg.)
  ISBN-10: 0-531-25354-6 (lib. bdg.)
  1. Japan—Juvenile literature. I. Title. II. Series.
  DS806.S575 2012
  952—dc22   2011009503

Japan

Contents

Cover photo:
Geisha at Fushimi Inari Taisha Shrine, Kyoto

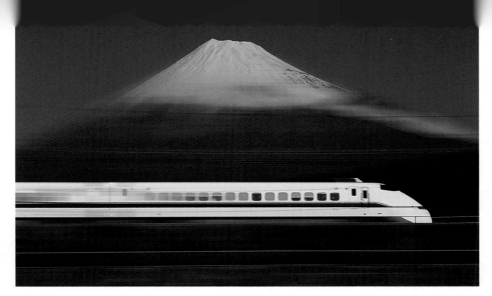

The Shinkansen, or bullet train

Sika deer

Mad for Manga

MASARU CAN HARDLY WAIT FOR THE SCHOOL DAY TO end. His elementary school has started a new club: manga art. After school, he has clubs four days a week and school chores on Tuesdays. Japanese schools do not hire janitors. It is up to the students to clean the school, a chore that is taken in turns. Today, cleaning the classroom is the last thing on Masaru's mind. It is manga day.

Like most children his age, Masaru is mad for manga. Every day Masaru, his father, and his older sister, Ako, read their favorite manga. In his club, Masaru is learning how to draw the dramatic eyes that dominate the faces of manga characters.

What is manga? Manga is a type of Japanese comic or printed cartoon. Most are black-and-white, although there are some full-color manga. Manga is big business in Japan, and both children and adults are devoted to their favorites. Pick any subject and there is a manga for it: history, romance, science fiction, fantasy, horror, mystery, and even business. There are manga drawn for girls, boys, teens, parents, and the

Opposite: **Boys in Tokyo race home after school.**

elderly. Today, manga publishing is a US$3.6 billion industry. Some manga, such as Pokémon, are now popular in the United States.

Ai and her family head for a long weekend in Kyoto. Their destination is the Kyoto International Manga Museum. The weekend offers Ai a rest from the pressures of *chugakko*, or junior high school. This is her last year in junior high, and she hopes to go to a top high school. To do so, she will need to do well on the entrance exam. For the past three years, her days have been filled with classes, clubs, and studying at a *juku*. A juku is a cram school, a special school geared to help students get into a good high school. Nights bring more studying and, just before bedtime, a chance to read her favorite manga.

At fourteen years old, Ai follows *shojo*, modern manga drawn for girls and women. Her favorite manga artist is Matsuri Hino. Ai reads Hino's two hit manga series, *MeruPuri*

The Father of Manga

Osamu Tezuka (1928–1989) founded Japan's manga and anime industries. Tezuka, often called "Japan's Walt Disney," developed the characteristic large eyes and wild hairstyles typical of manga characters. His most famous creation was Tetsuwan Atom, better known as AstroBoy. He also developed *Kimba the White Lion* and *Princess Knight*, both popular cartoon shows in the United States. Takarazuka, Japan, is home to the Osamu Tezuka Manga Museum, which was built to honor Tezuka.

and *Vampire Knight*. The Kyoto museum is hosting an exhibition of shojo, and Hino is presenting a class for future artists. Since Ai hopes to make her future in this art form, the chance to work with Hino is an honor.

The Kyoto International Manga Museum is one of several manga museums in Japan. The museum offers special exhibits, workshops, and lectures. Since it opened in 2006, the museum has collected more than three hundred thousand manga-related items. Visitors can ask to read very rare manga in the museum's reference room. The museum also has fifty thousand books in the Wall of Manga. Any visitor can take a book from the wall and read it.

The Kyoto International Manga Museum houses more than two hundred thousand comic books.

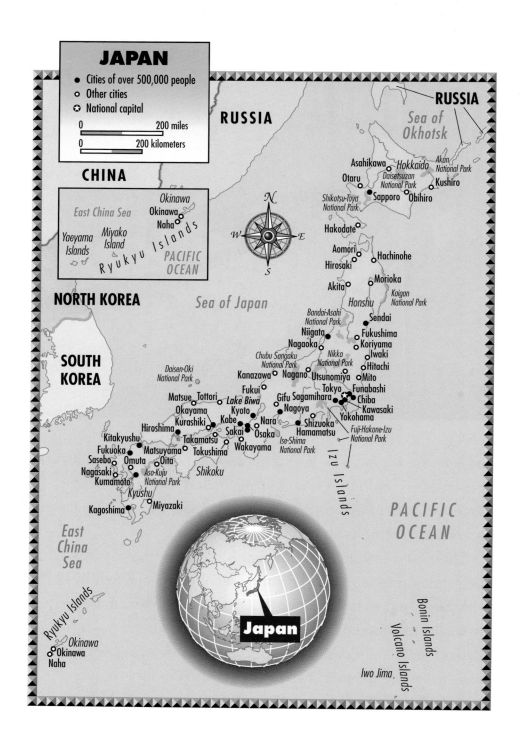

JAPAN

- ● Cities of over 500,000 people
- ○ Other cities
- ✪ National capital

0 — 200 miles
0 — 200 kilometers

RUSSIA

CHINA

NORTH KOREA

SOUTH KOREA

East China Sea

Okinawa
Okinawa
Naha

Yaeyama Islands

Miyako Island

Ryukyu Islands

PACIFIC OCEAN

Sea of Japan

RUSSIA

Sea of Okhotsk

Asahikawa
Otaru
Hokkaido
Daisetsuzan National Park
Akan National Park
Kushiro
Shikotsu-Toya National Park
Sapporo
Obihiro

Hakodate

Aomori
Hirosaki
Hachinohe

Akita
Morioka

Honshu
Kaigan National Park

Bandai-Asahi National Park
Sendai
Niigata
Fukushima
Nagaoka
Koriyama
Chubu Sangaku National Park
Nikko National Park
Iwaki
Kanazawa
Nagano
Utsunomiya
Hitachi
Fukui
Mito
Daisen-Oki National Park
Gifu Sagamihara
Tokyo
Funabashi
Matsue Tottori
Lake Biwa
Nagoya
Chiba
Okayama
Kyoto
Nara
Shizuoka
Kawasaki
Kurashiki
Kobe
Yokohama
Hiroshima
Sakai
Osaka
Hamamatsu
Fuji-Hakone-Izu National Park
Kitakyushu
Takamatsu
Wakayama
Ise-Shima National Park
Fukuoka
Matsuyama
Tokushima
Sasebo
Omuta
Oita
Nagasaki
Aso-Kuju National Park
Shikoku
Kumamoto
Kyushu

Kagoshima
Miyazaki

East China Sea

Ryukyu Islands

Okinawa
Okinawa
Naha

Izu Islands

PACIFIC OCEAN

Bonin Islands

Volcano Islands

Iwo Jima

Japan

Koji works in an anime studio. Anime is the animated version of manga. Many manga storylines have become television shows and video games. Koji, a fan of both manga and anime, is not an artist. He is an actor. The studio liked Koji's voice and cast him as a character in an anime TV show. Koji does voices for three different anime TV shows and for the video games that use the same characters.

The studio is a hive of activity. Rows of artists work at their computers producing the wide-eyed, wild-haired characters for six weekly anime series. The cast of each show keeps to a tight recording schedule, and musicians and singers come in regularly to perform new songs for the shows.

Teens and tots play manga-based video games. Young and old collect manga magazines and watch anime on television. In Japan, a love for manga spans all ages.

Pokémon

Whether it is TV cartoons, video games, trading cards, T-shirts, or one of the more than one thousand other Pokémon products, Pokémon continues to be one of Japan's most popular cartoons. Pokémon is everywhere. Japanese TV shows the cartoons and hosts a children's program on which contestants compete to become a Pokémon champion. The show opens with a song that lists all 150 Pokémon monsters—a single that became an instant hit on the Japanese music charts.

Land and
Sea

T WENTY MILLION YEARS AGO, FOUR GREAT LANDMASSES beneath the Pacific Ocean crashed together. A banana-shaped arc of land was pushed, pulled, and shoved along the edge of Asia. All this pushing and shoving created cracks, or faults, and searing lava poured from the openings. Out of all this activity came the islands we know today as Japan. Millions of years later, the islands still have volcanic activity. The faults still shift, causing earthquakes. The land that is Japan continues to move and change.

Japan has 6,852 islands, but only 426 have people living on them. Together, the islands make up an archipelago, a string of islands in the sea. The arc of islands runs 1,500 miles (2,400 kilometers) along the coast of Asia. The two nearest countries to Japan are Russia and South Korea. Only 100 miles (160 km) separate Japan and South Korea.

Japan covers a total area of 145,882 square miles (377,833 square kilometers), making it about the size of the state of Montana. Four islands make up the majority of the land. Honshu, the largest island, is mostly mountains, but it does have

Opposite: **Japan has the sixth-longest coastline of any country.**

How do Japan's four largest islands compare in size to states in the United States?

The island of...	Is about the same size as...
Honshu	Minnesota
Hokkaido	South Carolina
Kyushu	Maryland
Shikoku	Delaware

the Kanto and Nobi Plains, where the island's largest cities of Tokyo, Yokohama, Kyoto, and Osaka are found. Hokkaido lies north of Honshu. It is closest to the Arctic and cold in winter. Kyushu and Shikoku are much smaller islands. They lie south of Honshu.

Mountains, Rivers, and Lakes

Mountain ranges form the backbone of the Japanese islands. The highest mountain ranges are the Japanese Alps in the center of Honshu. Most of Japan's mountains are volcanoes. Some are dormant (sleeping) and others are active. Mount Fuji, in the heart of the Japanese Alps, is a volcano that has lain dormant for three hundred years. Most of Japan's islands are also mountains. They are the peaks of mountains that rise from the seafloor.

Rice fields blanket parts of Honshu.

Japan's Geographic Features

Area: 145,882 square miles (377,833 sq km)

Largest island: Honshu, 810 miles (1,300 km) long; 140 miles (230 km) wide

Largest city: Tokyo, population 13,010,279 (2010 est.)

Highest elevation: Mount Fuji, 12,388 feet (3,776 m) above sea level

Lowest elevation: Hachiro-gata, 13 feet (4 m) below sea level

Longest river: Shinano River, 228 miles (367 km)

Largest lake: Lake Biwa, 259 square miles (670 sq km)

Most active volcano: Mount Aso

Lowest recorded temperature: −42°F (−41°C) in Asahikawa, on January 25, 1902

Highest recorded temperature: 105.6°F (40.9°C) in Tajimi, Gifu, on August 16, 2007

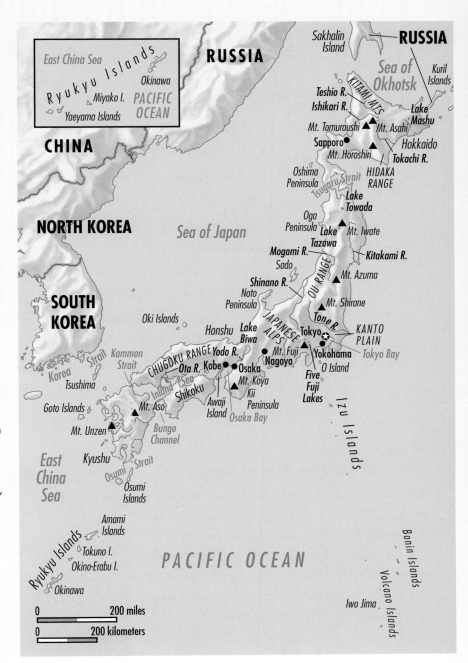

Japan's rivers rush down mountainsides, pour over waterfalls, and cut through deep, rocky valleys. Large ships cannot navigate these shallow, swift rivers. The country's longest river is the Shinano, which runs 228 miles (367 km) from Nagano to Niigata. The Shinano rises on Mount Kobushi and empties into the Sea of Japan.

In Japan, lakes fill craters of sleeping volcanoes and narrow mountain gorges. Mount Fuji's Five Lakes are smooth as glass and icy cold, like a string of crystals in a necklace. Lava dammed a river, forming this chain of lakes. Lake Toya formed when the caldera, or bowl, of a sleeping volcano filled with rainwater and snowmelt. Lake Biwa, Japan's largest lake, covers about 259 square miles (670 sq km). The lake, located on Honshu near Kyoto, is believed to be about four million years old. Every year about five thousand waterbirds arrive at Lake Biwa. They wade along the lake's edge, feeding on fish and crustaceans.

Fuji-san, the Roof of Japan

Fuji-san, or Mount Fuji, is Japan's highest mountain, rising 12,388 feet (3,776 m) above sea level. It is named for the Buddhist fire goddess Fuchi and is revered by the Japanese people. Buddhist legend claims that Fuji emerged from the earth in 286 BCE. On a clear day, Mount Fuji can be seen from Tokyo, which is about 60 miles (100 km) away.

Volcanoes, Earthquakes, and Tsunamis

A ring of active volcanoes known as the Ring of Fire encircles the Pacific Ocean. All of Japan and its 108 active volcanoes make up part of this ring. Japan has one-tenth of the world's active volcanoes. Although Fuji has not erupted since 1707, the Japan Meteorological Agency (JMA) still considers it an active volcano. The JMA keeps a close eye on thirty volcanoes, including Shinmoedake, Aso, Miyakejima, and Usu, all of which have erupted in recent years.

Steamy Onsen

An *onsen* is a hot spring. Underground water is heated by molten rock below the earth's surface. When the water comes to the surface, it can form pools that are hot enough to cook an egg. Sometimes hot steam rises into the air, leaving towns under a constant white veil.

Volcanic activity is closely related to earthquakes. Many of Japan's volcanoes lie on or near fault lines. As pressure from beneath the earth's surface builds, the rock along fault lines slips and slides. Most of the time, these shifts are so small that people do not feel them. Sometimes, the ground trembles, buildings tumble, and loud rumbling is heard for miles around. Some years, the earth under Japan stays fairly quiet. In other years, Japanese citizens feel up to two thousand earthquakes.

One of Japan's worst earthquakes took place in 1923 near Tokyo. Called the Great Kanto earthquake, it killed more than one hundred and forty thousand people. Fewer people die in earthquakes today because buildings are constructed to withstand them. Local governments regularly hold drills to prepare people for massive earthquakes. In 2011, a magnitude 9.0 earthquake hit underwater off the coast of Sendai. It was the most powerful earthquake ever recorded in Japan, and it set off a devastating tsunami.

Tsunamis are huge waves that can occur after an earthquake happens beneath the ocean. The word *tsunami* means "harbor wave" in Japanese. The undersea event pushes ocean water in all directions at once. Some tsunami waves move as fast as 600 miles per hour (1,000 km). By the time they crash ashore, the waves are sometimes 100 feet (30 m) high. They hit with incredible force and wash away everything in their way. Because tsunamis can be so deadly, coastal towns have tsunami warning systems to protect their citizens.

Disaster Strikes

On the afternoon of March 11, 2011, people in Japan were going about their everyday lives. They were at work. They were at school. But then the earth began to shake, and it kept shaking for six minutes. A massive 9.0 earthquake had hit off the coast of Sendai. It was the fifth most powerful earthquake the world had experienced since modern recordkeeping began in 1900.

Although the earthquake caused some damage, it was the tsunami that followed that was the true disaster. About an hour after the quake, a wave that was 30 feet (10 m) high in some places crashed ashore. The rushing water swept away cars, trucks, and airplanes. It wiped out entire towns. It also severely damaged a nuclear power plant, sending dangerous radiation into the air and water. An estimated twenty-five thousand people died in the earthquake and tsunami. The effects from radiation exposure to humans, plants, and animals won't be fully known for years.

A Look at Japan's Cities

Located on the western coast of Tokyo Bay, Yokohama (2010 estimated population: 3,654,427) is a major shipping center. It is the second-largest city in Japan, trailing only the capital of Tokyo. Yokohama and Tokyo have expanded so much that they have grown together and are now like one large city. The Yokohama Marine Tower is the tallest inland lighthouse in the world.

Osaka (population: 2,668,113) is one of the economic centers of Japan. It has long been important in the nation. In 645 CE, when it was known by the name Naniwa, it became Japan's first capital city. The oldest Buddhist temple in Japan, Shitenno-ji, was built in Osaka in 593 CE. Today, the city is known for its many parks, including Tennoji Park, which houses a zoo, an art museum, and a Japanese garden.

Nagoya (population: 2,258,804) is home to several beautiful castles, shrines, and art museums. Tourists flock to the Nagoya Castle (above), built in 1612, and Atsuta Shrine, one of Japan's most revered shrines.

The host of the 1972 Winter Olympics, Sapporo (population: 1,905,777) is the place to go for winter sports or relaxing summer holidays. The annual Snow Festival (left) draws skiers and snowboarders, but many people come just to see the amazing snow sculptures. In June, the Yosakoi Soran Festival hosts several hundred dancing and singing teams.

Typhoon winds whip palm trees in Okinawa.

From Subtropical to Subarctic

Japan's climate changes from island to island, and from one side of an island to the other. On the eastern side of Honshu, spring brings monsoon rains to drench city streets. A monsoon is a strong wind that blows in from the ocean, usually bringing heavy rainfall. In some areas, total rainfall for a year reaches 70 inches (180 centimeters). As summer dries the rain-soaked earth, typhoon season approaches. A typhoon is the same thing as a hurricane, except it occurs in the northwest Pacific Ocean. Japanese people expect strong winds, heavy rain, and flooding from high waves when a typhoon strikes. In winter, snow blankets the Japanese landscape.

Name Your Typhoon

Typhoons can strike fourteen Pacific Ocean nations, each located north of the equator. Each country affected submits a list of names, which are used in rotation. The names may be flowers, animals, star signs, or personal names. The names submitted by Japan include Usagi, Koppu, and Tokage.

Japan is a long, thin nation. In all, it has six distinct climate zones: Hokkaido, Sea of Japan, Central Highland, Seto Inland Sea, Pacific Ocean, and Southwest Island. Hokkaido experiences cool summers with average temperatures around 72 degrees Fahrenheit (22 degrees Celsius). Winter weather has a distinct Arctic influence. Temperatures drop, and snowstorms are frequent. Arctic winds also affect the Sea of

In winter, heavy snow blankets Hokkaido and much of Honshu.

Japan climate zone. Monsoon winds from December to March carry cold air and bring heavy snow. The Seto Inland Sea region enjoys a mild climate all year with very little rainfall. The Pacific Ocean climate is the climate of eastern Honshu. Southwestern islands have extremely mild winters and hot, humid summers.

A strong, warm ocean current, called the Kuroshio (Japan Current), passes the southern half of Japan, keeping the islands warm and wet. From the north, the Kuril Current flows southward from the Bering Sea. When the warm waters of the Kuroshio meet the Arctic waters of the Kuril, dense sea fog occurs. During the summer, the east coast of Hokkaido is covered with thick fog.

In summer, fog often settles over Lake Mashu on Hokkaido.

Students pose next to recycling bins. Japanese law requires schools to recycle glass, plastic, paper, and aluminum.

Conservation

Because Japan covers a small area but has a large population, conserving the environment has become a crucial issue. Factories once filled the air with pollution. Neighborhoods expanded into the countryside, taking over wildlife habitats. Rivers were choked by chemicals used to make plants grow and kill pests.

A large population like Japan uses massive amounts of water and produces great amounts of garbage. The Japanese have become highly efficient at conserving water. They have water-saving toilets, take baths using minimal amounts of water, and avoid wasting water. Recycling is important in Japan. Homes, schools, and businesses recycle all paper, glass, metal, cardboard, and plastic. Recycling is not just good for the environment, it is the law. Since 2000, the amount of plastic that is recycled has increased by 464 percent.

Although Japanese factories must filter all air- and water-polluting agents, Japan cannot control what happens in neighboring countries. Air pollution in China and Korea creates acid rain. The rain has so much acid that it kills plants. Japan invited nations from around the world to discuss the problems of air pollution and climate change. One hundred and forty-one nations have signed the Kyoto Protocol to reduce air pollution. The United States is not one of those nations.

Fumes from factories and cars are often dangerous for the environment.

Boars, Birds, and Blossoms

A SMALL BLACK RABBIT WITH EXTREMELY SHORT EARS browses on low-lying ferns. This is the Amami rabbit, which lives in old-growth forests on the islands of Amami Oshima and Tokuno-shima. The Amami rabbit is an endangered species. It was once hunted for food and for use as an ingredient in folk medicine. Although protected from human hunting, stray dogs and cats and Indian mongooses continue to threaten the rabbit's survival.

Islands, by their very nature, become individual ecosystems, often home to unique animals such as the Amami rabbit. At some point, animals arrive on an island. They may travel across a land bridge or be brought by humans. They may float across the sea on logs or seaweed or fly to the island. Once there, animals adjust to the amount of rainfall or dryness, to heat or cold. They learn to live on the food. They may have no way to leave the island, and so they develop into a new species adapted to a new environment. Since Japan is made up of so many islands, different animals and plants have evolved, or developed, on each one.

Opposite: **Hibiscus flowers bloom on Ishigaki Island.**

Japan's islands host 188 species of mammals and more than 660 types of birds. Many of the birds spend only winters in Japan, moving to the Arctic during the summer nesting season. Fifty-nine different amphibians live on the islands, from tiny Japanese tree frogs to giant Japanese salamanders that can weigh up to 55 pounds (25 kilograms). Reptiles on the islands include mainly snakes and tortoises or sea turtles.

Wild Animals

With such a large human population, many of Japan's wildlife habitats have been destroyed to make way for houses, office buildings, and parks. But many animals, such as macaques and wild boars, still find homes in the mountain forests and in remote areas of the islands.

Iriomote Cats

The island of Iriomote is the only habitat of the Iriomote cat. The cats, which are about the size of a house cat, are light brown with rows of dark brown spots. Fierce predators, Iriomote cats hunt fruit bats, wild pigs, rats, fish, birds, and insects. The population of this species may be as low as one hundred. They are endangered because human development has destroyed much of the habitat on their small island home.

Japan is home to more sika deer than any other country in the world.

Once, rice paddies—the flooded fields where rice is grown—provided ideal homes for Japanese critters. More than six hundred species of birds visit Japan as they travel between their winter homes and summer nesting places. Many birds—egrets, herons, cranes, and storks—rested and fed in rice paddies. Frogs and snakes, freshwater fish, and snails lived in paddy waters, while dragonflies and damselflies laid their eggs in the slim stalks of the rice plants. Heavy use of fertilizers and pesticides has killed off many paddy-dwelling animals. In addition, the process of draining the paddies helps farmers but destroys the natural habitat of animals that need the water to live.

There are not many large mammal species in Japan, but the country does have bears, wild boars, sika deer, and serow antelopes. Japanese macaques live farther north than any of their monkey or ape relatives.

It is not hard to find reptiles on Japan's many islands. Sea turtles lay their eggs on beaches of the southernmost islands. Lakes and ponds provide homes for tortoises and lizards. Japan has two fairly common venomous snakes, the Japanese pit viper and the Japanese grass snake. Other venomous snakes, called *habu*, live on small islands, where there are few humans. Newts, frogs, and toads thrive around small streams and ponds, but the Japanese giant salamander is becoming rare. In the past, the Japanese hunted giant salamanders for food, but laws now protect them.

The Tancho of Kushiro

Saving the *tancho*, also known as the red-crowned crane, is an important conservation effort in Japan. The Kushiro Marsh, nesting ground of the tancho, became a national park in 1987 in an effort to protect the magnificent cranes. According to ancient legend, the tancho lived for a thousand years. The bird symbolizes long life and good fortune.

Macaques Take a Dip

In 1963, a young female macaque waded into a hot spring in the Nagano Mountains to get some soybeans thrown there by a ranger. Since then, troops of macaques have been enjoying warm dips in the hot springs. These playful monkeys' natural habitat ranges from northwest Honshu to Oshima Island.

Macaques have shown other surprising behaviors. Some macaques wash potatoes in the sea. Scientists left potatoes on a beach for the macaques. The clever monkeys washed the sand off the potatoes in the sea and discovered that the food tasted better dipped in saltwater. Now, they dip their potatoes in the water between bites.

Habitat protection is a key element in the survival of Japan's wildlife. Marshes and bogs provide homes for many animals, but those areas can be drained for human use as well. Red-crowned cranes, whooper swans, and Steller's sea eagles all winter in Japan and are struggling to survive because their habitats are being taken for farmland or industrial needs. Japan has set up twenty-nine national parks, which provide some protected habitats, but the parks are small.

As more land is taken for housing, wild animals look for food and shelter where they can find it. Many animals, including endangered macaques, invade farmland and munch on crops. Tanuki, or raccoon dogs, raid garbage cans and steal eggs from chicken farms. Trapping and hunting sometimes help with these problems, but they can also create conservation problems. The Japanese have a long tradition of respect for wild animals. The government is trying to balance human needs with conservation needs, but it is not easy.

Japanese Plants

Japan's varied climates produce conditions that support an exceptionally wide variety of plants. Japan has about seven thousand species of trees, flowers, shrubs, and ferns. About twenty-nine hundred are native to Japan.

Many islands have semitropical rain forests. Ferns cover the forest floors with lacy green fronds. Mulberry trees and oaks stretch toward the sky, and vines curl up around tree trunks. Bamboo grows wild in thick, straight clusters. Hibiscus blooms flash brilliant reds and pinks against the lush green of the rain forests.

Plum blossoms are among the first blossoms to appear in the spring. Near Tokyo, they sometimes bloom as early as February.

The National Tree

Sugi is sometimes called the Japanese cedar, but it is not related to the cedar at all. Sugi are large evergreens that grow up to 230 feet (70 m) tall and have trunks 13 feet (4 m) thick. The national tree of Japan, sugi is commonly planted around Buddhist and Shinto temples. Many sugi have lived for centuries.

Japan's temperate forests are filled with evergreens. Holly, Japanese evergreen oaks, laurel, and pasania grow in the lowlands. As the elevation increases, the types of trees change to cedars, red and black pines, and a host of broad-leafed trees. In the fall, the mountains come alive with color as Japanese maple leaves turn to vivid red, against the yellows of birches and deep golds of larches.

Japan's forests boast a number of flowering trees that fill the springtime woods with color. The first signs of spring are *ume* blossoms, which cover plum tree branches with deep pink flowers. A few weeks later, *sakura*, Japanese cherry trees, bloom in shades ranging from nearly white to baby pink to a rich rose pink. Although many people consider cherry blossoms a symbol of Japan, few Japanese plant cherry trees in their yards. The blooms are too short-lived for true beauty, so many Japanese prefer the year-round beauty of evergreens.

A Long and Honored History

SOMETIME BETWEEN 35,000 AND 30,000 YEARS AGO, humans arrived on the islands of Japan. Although a sea separates Japan from mainland Asia, that was not always the case. At one point, a land bridge connected Japan to present-day Russia. Hungry hunter-gatherers followed great woolly mammoths and other game across the land bridge to Japan.

The Early People

How early humans fared in Japan remains a mystery. There are no written records of the time, but historians have found stone tools, animal remains, and the bones of humans from early times.

The first organized culture of Japan was the Jomon culture, which flourished from 8000 to 300 BCE. The Jomon people hunted game animals, fished, and gathered fruits, seeds, and nuts for food. Family groups traveled from place to place searching for food. They made tools from stone and an early type of cord-wrapped pottery.

Around 300 BCE, the Yayoi era began. This society

Opposite: **This warrior figure was made around 500 CE. It was placed in the earth as part of a burial ritual.**

Queen Himiko

According to Chinese records, Queen Himiko rose to power during the Yayoi era. She is said to have lived in a fortress on a hill with a thousand young female servants to tend to her needs. Himiko herself did not govern her people. She left that job to her brother. Instead, she served as a spiritual leader.

advanced to planting and harvesting rice. To work the fields and harvest crops, people had to remain in one place. Small villages sprouted wherever farming was possible. Family groups began trading with each other. Language developed. By about 100 CE, people who looked and spoke like today's Japanese lived on many of Japan's islands.

The Ainu

The northernmost island of Hokkaido is the home of the Ainu. These are native people of Japan. Their existence is linked to the Jomon culture, which existed as long ago as 8000 BCE. The Ainu culture emerged in the 1200s BCE. They hunted game; gathered wild fruits, nuts, and other plant parts; and trapped animals for their fur. Historians believe that the furs were used to trade with other cultures, particularly to acquire iron tools and pots. Fewer than twenty thousand Ainu survive today.

Horyu-ji, a Buddhist temple at Nara, is one of the oldest wooden buildings in the world. It dates to 670 CE.

Early Kingdoms

Around 300 CE, most of Japan came under the rule of powerful clans, groups of people descended from a common relative. These clans, called *uji*, had specific territories. The Yamatos became influential near present-day Osaka. The Yamatos saw value in learning from other cultures, and they developed ties with Korea and China. A clear class system, much like social classes in China, developed with rulers, skilled craftspeople, farmers, peasants, and enslaved people.

This was a period of learning. Foreigners brought their knowledge of the Chinese writing system. With changes over time, character writing became Japan's written language. Along with language, the Koreans brought the teachings of Buddha, an important philosopher.

Great change was coming. In 593 CE, Empress Suiko appointed her nephew Prince Shotoku regent, meaning he would rule in her place. As Japan's substitute ruler, Prince Shotoku believed that Japan could advance by following the ways of Chinese culture. He invited skilled Chinese tradespeople to work in Japan. New buildings took on a Chinese appearance. Shotoku admired Buddhism and encouraged Japanese citizens to follow the teachings of Buddha.

Shotoku gave Japan its first written constitution, called the Seventeen Article Constitution. This document became Japan's first written

Prince Shotoku and his two sons. Shotoku held power from 593 CE until his death in 622 CE.

laws. The articles called for harmony among the people and following Buddhist ideals. Citizens were expected to obey the commands of their ruler, who would treat them with kindness and respect. Shotoku urged the people to punish evil and reward good. He required the Japanese people to not be jealous of others.

The Nara Period

During the Nara period (710–794 CE), Japan established a permanent capital city in Nara. The city's buildings and layout were based on the Chinese city of Xi'an. The people followed Buddhist teachings, and Chinese writing and art flourished.

The noble class became particularly interested in the arts. Sculptors produced statues of Buddha, and the government built forty-eight temples within the capital city. The first collection of Japanese poetry, called *Manyoshu, A Collection of Ten Thousand Leaves*, was published at this time.

The Land of the Rising Sun

Prince Shotoku is considered the source of Japan's name as the "rising sun" or *Nihon*. In a letter to the Chinese emperor, Shotoku said, "The Emperor of the land where the sun rises sends a letter to the Emperor of the land where the sun sets. How are you?"

Nara was an artistic center. This silk tapestry made in Nara depicts paradise.

Manyoshu, A Collection of Ten Thousand Leaves

The first book of poetry published in Japan contained forty-five hundred poems. Many were tanka, five-line poems with thirty-one syllables in the pattern of 5-7-5-7-7 syllables. It is very easy to make rhymes in the Japanese language, so Japanese people make poetry by counting syllables instead. More than 450 poets contributed their work to *Manyoshu*. The remarkable thing about the collection is the variety of people who contributed. They include men and women, nobles and commoners, farmers, entertainers, and civil servants.

The Heian Period

In 794 CE, Emperor Kammu moved the capital from Nara to Heian, a city known now as Kyoto. Kammu controlled the nation, and all power lay in the capital. The Heian era (794–1185 CE) was a time of art and learning. Gentlemen of the court hunted and enjoyed music and poetry. Noble ladies wrote women's literature about romance and courtly love. Women learned art, flower arranging, and calligraphy (fine handwriting).

Away from the capital, regional lords were busy acquiring large blocks of land. As each lord took more land, he also gained the farmers who worked the land. The lords collected

Poetry has long been an important art form in Japan. This twelfth-century scroll shows scholars reading a poem.

taxes from all the workers, who provided crops, work, and military service to their lord. The lords hired professional soldiers, called samurai, for protection of their lands and property. They, in turn, paid the samurai with land. Samurai became rich, and Japan became a land of warriors.

Feudal Lords and Private Armies

As the samurai became stronger, the emperor and his court grew weaker. The true power in Japan rested in the hands of the landowners. Samurai who served Japan were granted more land as their wages. In 1192, Minamoto Yoritomo became the shogun, a warrior governor, and founded the Kamakura shogunate.

Japan's economy was changing. Farmers used horses and plows to till their lands. Waterwheels made it possible to water the crops and increase crop yields. With better farming

The Age of the Samurai

The samurai were highly educated warriors who were loyal to their overlords, called shoguns. From the 1200s to the 1500s, samurai were skilled in the use of the *katana* (sword) and the *yumi* (a type of bow). During the Tokugawa era (1600–1867), the samurai represented the highest class in Japanese society. Two and a half centuries of peace turned the samurai from fierce warriors into government officials. Samurai government ended in 1868, when a group of young reformers seized control of the country in the name of young Emperor Meiji.

Japanese samurai fight off the invading Mongol army.

practices, farmers raised two crops a year. The main crop was rice, and farmers gave about one-third of their crops for land tax. Farmers began developing manufacturing skills to earn extra money. They raised silkworms and wove the silk into cloth. They made paper, built furniture, and paid their taxes by giving those products to their lords.

In 1274, Mongols under Kublai Khan, a powerful leader whose empire stretched across much of mainland Asia, tried to invade Japan. A storm destroyed many of their ships and forced the Mongols to turn back. The next year, they tried to cross the sea and were met by a fierce storm, called a *kamikaze*. The Mongol army finally arrived and entered into battle. Although the samurai defeated the Mongols, they were unhappy with the way their leader had coped with the attack. As happened so many times in Japan's history, the decline of one clan made room for the rise of another.

By the 1330s, the Ashikaga clan had defeated the ruling Minamotos. The Ashikaga shogun, Takauji (1305–1358),

Last Name First

Traditionally, Japanese family names come first, and the given names follow. In this book, most names are written English-style, with family names last. The names from the unification period are an exception. Because most books and online sources refer to them in the traditional way, with last name first, this book does as well.

grew bold with success. Takauji led Japan into a new era, the Ashikaga period, which lasted from 1336 to 1573. Then Japan entered a period of civil war that lasted for decades. Lords and samurai struggled to become the new shogun who would reunite Japan.

At the end of the sixteenth century, three daimyos, or great lords, arose to put an end to the warring and unite Japan. Those men were Oda Nobunaga (1534–1582), Toyotomi

Oda Nobunaga was considered a brave and inventive leader.

Hideyoshi (1536–1598), and Tokugawa Ieyasu (1543–1616).
They are called the Three Unifiers. In the midst of warring
shoguns, Oda Nobunaga proved to be a brilliant military
thinker. By the time he was twenty-six years old, Nobunaga
had inherited his father's estate and united the province of
Owari under his rule.

In 1562, Nobunaga and Ieyasu, a neighboring shogun,
became military allies who supported each other in the event
of an attack. Nobunaga hoped to unite all of Japan under one
ruler and stop the endless warring. Unfortunately, he did not
live long enough to see his dream fulfilled. A close servant
of Nobunaga's, Akechi Mitsuhide, ambushed and murdered
Nobunaga before he could complete the reunification of Japan.

Hideyoshi, a foot soldier in Nobunaga's army, served his
lord well. He became a samurai and followed Nobunaga's

orders fully. In 1577, Hideyoshi led Nobunaga's soldiers against warlike daimyos in western Japan. When he heard about Nobunaga's death, Hideyoshi quickly stopped his fight in the west and returned to Owari. He broke the small revolt Akechi Mitsuhide had stirred up and took Mitsuhide's head in the process. Hideyoshi then installed Nobunaga's grandson as head of the estate. Controlling the child, Hideyoshi became the most powerful man in the country and real successor to Nobunaga. It was Hideyoshi who reunified Japan, forcing all the remaining independent daimyos to bow down to him.

The Edo Period

Hideyoshi died leaving only young children. Nobunaga's old ally, Tokugawa Ieyasu, defeated his rivals in 1600. He founded a shogun dynasty that would rule over a peaceful and prosperous Japan for two and a half centuries.

Tokugawa Ieyasu

Tokugawa Ieyasu (1543–1616) was one of Japan's greatest military leaders. When he was born, Japan was in the midst of violent feuding between powerful clans. He lived for years as a hostage at an enemy's court to ensure peace between the two clans. By the late 1500s, political scheming had reached a fever pitch, and civil war broke out again. In 1600, he led Emperor Go-Yozei's army against the fierce Western Army and won. Go-Yozei honored Ieyasu by naming him a shogun, a military governor.

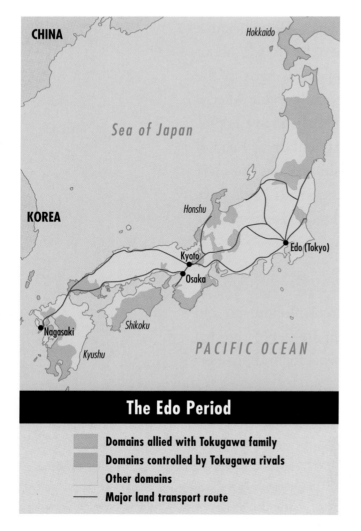

The Edo Period

- Domains allied with Tokugawa family
- Domains controlled by Tokugawa rivals
- Other domains
- —— Major land transport route

Japan was undergoing a period of great change. A slow shift in the population began with the rise of industry. Cities grew, and people were drawn to higher wages in factories. Some cities grew faster than others, and Edo (Tokyo) grew from a small fishing village to a city of more than a million people by the mid-eighteenth century.

During the Edo period (1600–1867), people moved into cities, and workers and the middle class were no longer burdened by constant labor. In their free time, people wanted entertainment. Music, storytelling, Kabuki theater, and Bunraku (large puppets) drew large audiences. People became interested in art and literature, particularly poetry. The poet Matsuo Basho became known as a master of the haiku, a three-line poem of seventeen syllables.

During this time, Japan remained isolated from the rest of the world. Foreigners were discouraged from visiting. Japanese rulers feared that too much contact with the Western world would destroy Japan's culture. Western countries were collecting colonies around the world, and the Japanese feared they would be next.

In 1853, U.S. Navy boats under the command of Commodore Matthew Perry arrived in Edo Bay. Perry's ships were steamships, a new and frightening sight for the Japanese, who thought the ships were giant dragons puffing smoke. Nine months after Perry's arrival, the United States forced Japan to sign a treaty that opened Japanese ports to American trade.

Commodore Matthew Perry met with Japanese officials in 1853.

The Meiji Restoration

The Japanese were not sure how best to deal with the foreigners in order to keep Japan free. In 1868, a group of young samurai led a revolution that put the Meiji emperor in power. This began the era of the Meiji restoration (1868–1912).

When Meiji began his reign, Japan had little military strength. The economy was based on agriculture, and there was little industry. Meiji insisted on a constitution that established a more modern form of government. Meiji modeled his new government on the British system. The emperor remained the supreme ruler, but the people now had a voice in government through the House of Representatives. There was also a House of Peers, made up of members of the imperial family and other nobles. The samurai class was eliminated. Private armies were disbanded, and Japan became a united nation.

A train crosses a bay at Takanawa. The first railroad in Japan was built in 1872.

The economy slowly shifted from being totally driven by agriculture to a rise in industry. Textile mills and factories sprang up in the cities. Banks opened, and the yen became Japan's money system. A solid middle class rose, made up of factory owners, merchants, and government employees. In the 1870s, Meiji built a network of railroads, making it easier to transport crops, food, people, and manufactured goods throughout the country. Meiji also insisted that people follow the Shinto faith instead of Buddhism.

Not everyone was thrilled with Meiji's changes. In 1877, a group of samurai banded together in the Satsuma Rebellion. The Satsuma clan, from the island of Kyushu, resented the growth of the emperor's power and the loss of their own. Saigo Takamori led the samurai against a government army made up of peasants. Saigo did not think these people were capable or worthy of combat. But the government army, modeled on more modern European armies, had better weapons. The government force crushed the rebellion.

Meiji's military grew in experience and became a skilled war machine. By 1895, Japan had defeated China in several battles around Korea. Once Japan had a foothold in Korea, there was no stopping its powerful influence. In 1905, Japan won a major war against Russia over strategic locations in Manchuria, the northeastern part of China. Japan's growing nation needed raw materials, and Manchuria offered timber, minerals, and workers. The Japanese victory was the first time in modern history that a non-European nation had defeated a European nation. People around the world were shocked to see how strong Japan had become.

Japanese troops land in Korea in 1904.

In 1910, Japan made Korea its colony. Military leaders became even more powerful, and the Japanese entered into a period of industrial growth with one idea in mind. They hoped for Japan to take over most of Asia.

A World at War

World War I (1914–1918) spread from Europe into Asia, and Japan fought against Germany on the side of the Allies— Great Britain, France, the United States, and others. With no orders from the government, Japan's navy seized German-held islands in the Pacific. Japan went to the peace talks on the side of the winners.

Japanese soldiers in Russia. Between 1918 and 1922, seventy thousand Japanese troops were sent to Russia to try to stop the Russian Revolution.

Japan joined the League of Nations, a group of countries hoping to work out a lasting peace. Pacific islands taken during the war became permanent territories of Japan. Growing military power and a weak government gave the Japanese military more influence. Under this new military leadership, Japan invaded Manchuria in 1931. It set up a new independent state called Manchukuo, ruled by the last Chinese emperor, Pu Yi. Emperor Pu Yi was a weak puppet leader, and Japan's military pulled the puppet's strings. The Japanese presence in Manchukuo served as a staging ground for Japan's future plans in Asia. In 1933, Japan resigned from the League of Nations. The league's members did not agree with Japan's actions in Manchuria. Japan would not let other nations tell it what to do.

Far to the west, Germany elected Adolf Hitler as leader. Japan and Germany signed an agreement. In 1937, Japan

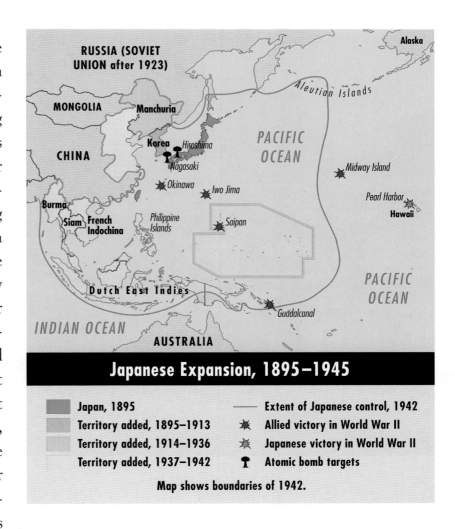

Japanese Expansion, 1895–1945

Japan, 1895	—— Extent of Japanese control, 1942
Territory added, 1895–1913	✳ Allied victory in World War II
Territory added, 1914–1936	✳ Japanese victory in World War II
Territory added, 1937–1942	♟ Atomic bomb targets

Map shows boundaries of 1942.

Japan's attack on Pearl Harbor damaged more than a dozen U.S. Navy ships and nearly two hundred aircraft.

invaded China, and two years later Germany invaded Poland. World War II had begun. This time, Japan was on the side of Germany and Italy.

On December 7, 1941, the Japanese navy bombed Pearl Harbor, Hawaii, then a territory of the United States, in a surprise attack. Admiral Isoroku Yamamoto, the commander of the Japanese forces that bombed Pearl Harbor, said about the attack, "I fear all we have done is to awaken a sleeping giant and fill him with a terrible resolve." He proved right.

Up to this point, the United States had stayed out of World War II, but Japanese actions changed American minds. The United States fought the war in both Asia and Europe. After four years of hard-fought battles, U.S. president Harry Truman issued an order to drop an atomic bomb on Hiroshima, Japan, on August 6, 1945. Three days later, the United States dropped a second atomic bomb on Nagasaki. Atomic bombs were the most destructive weapons the world had ever seen. The twin bombings killed more than two hundred thousand people. With two major cities devastated, Japan surrendered on August 14, 1945.

As part of the peace agreement, Japan lost its overseas territories in the Pacific. The state of Manchukuo returned to being Manchuria under Chinese rule. Korea gained independence from Japan, and Taiwan ceased to be a Japanese colony. Russia occupied Sakhalin Island and the Kuril Islands, which had also been under Japanese rule.

Emperor Hirohito

Emperor Hirohito (1901–1989) became imperial Japan's crown prince in 1916 at the age of fifteen. After graduating from school, he traveled throughout Europe. When his father, Emperor Yoshihito, became sick, Hirohito needed to take control of the empire. When Japan lost the war, Hirohito lost all real political power. From 1945 until his death, Hirohito pursued his interest in marine biology.

General Douglas MacArthur (third from left) oversaw the U.S. occupation of Japan.

After the War

The U.S. Army occupied Japan for seven years after the war ended. Under General Douglas MacArthur, the army brought about many changes. Japan's once-powerful military was taken apart. A new constitution set up a democratic monarchy. Japan's emperor went from being a powerful leader to a powerless figurehead. Women gained the right to vote, as political power shifted from the emperor to the people. Under the constitution, Japan could not maintain an army or go to war again, except to defend itself.

In the years after the war, Japan quickly developed into an economic power. It became a world leader in the manufacture of cars, electronic goods, and steel. Trade soared, as Japan sold goods in the United States and across Europe. In 1966, Toyota introduced the Corolla, the best-selling car of all time, and by the 1970s Japan had the world's second-largest economy, trailing only the United States.

Cities flourished, and some people thought the good times would never end. Prices on real estate went up and up and up. Then, in 1991, the bubble burst. Japanese people lost confidence in the future and stopped buying goods. The economy shrank. In the years that followed, Japan was further shaken by financial and political scandals. In the early years of the twenty-first century, the Japanese economy grew slowly. Workers, especially young people, remained uncertain about the future.

Motorcycles line the shop floor of the Yamaha factory in Tokyo. Japan became a major manufacturer of cars, trucks, and motorcycles in the second half of the twentieth century.

An Empire, a Democracy

JAPAN HAS THE WORLD'S OLDEST MONARCHY, BUT ITS government system is less than sixty-five years old. Up until 1947, when Japan's current constitution established a parliamentary government, an emperor ruled the nation. One hundred and twenty-five emperors have served as Japan's monarch.

The Japanese monarchy is called the Chrysanthemum Throne, and the emperor who sits on the throne is the world's only remaining emperor. Akihito is Japan's emperor, but he is not the true leader of Japan. The leader of Japan is the prime minister.

The Constitution

The Meiji Constitution of the Empire of Japan, written in 1889, was Japan's first constitution. That document set up a two-house parliament, called the Diet. The emperor appointed a cabinet, which consisted of noble leaders and advisers. At the time, only about 5 percent of the male population was allowed to vote. In 1925, all adult men were given the right to vote, but women could not vote.

Opposite: **Japan's lawmakers meet in the National Diet Building in Tokyo.**

Emperor Akihito

The current emperor, Akihito (1933–), is a member of the oldest imperial family in the world. He became emperor in 1989, after his father's death. He is married to a commoner, now Empress Michiko. They have three children, Prince Naruhito, Prince Akishino, and Princess Sayako. Each emperor's reign is given a title, and Akihito's reign is called Heisei, or "Achieving Peace."

After World War II ended in 1945, the United States military occupied Japan. In 1947, the United States insisted on a new constitution to replace the Meiji Constitution. The 1947 constitution guaranteed human rights, such as free speech, freedom of the press, and freedom of religion. Adults twenty years old and older, both men and women, had the right to vote. The Diet would be the main power in Japan, and the emperor would keep his title but have no power. The Japanese government would have three branches, the Diet (legislative), the cabinet (executive), and the courts (judicial). Tokyo would be Japan's capital city.

Sometimes called the Peace Constitution, the document states that Japan does not have the "right to wage war except to defend themselves if attacked." It also denies Japan the right to develop a large army or navy. Changes to this constitution require a two-thirds majority vote in both houses of the Diet, followed by a majority vote of the Japanese people.

The Diet

Japan's legislative branch, the Diet, is the most powerful branch of the Japanese government. It is based on the British Parliament and has two houses, the House of Councillors and the House of Representatives. Members of the Diet represent several different political parties. Japan has two main political parties, the

Members of the Democratic Party of Japan hold a meeting.

Tokyo: Japan's Capital City

Tokyo was founded in about 645 CE as a small fishing village. It was known as Edo. Over the years, Edo grew and grew, and by the middle of the 1800s, it was home to more than a million people. In 1868, it became the capital, and its name was changed to Tokyo.

In 2010, Tokyo had an estimated population of 13,010,279. Japan's second-largest city, Yokohama, sits right next to Tokyo. The two cities and their suburbs are the largest metropolitan area in the world with a population of about 35,676,000. Tokyo is the heart of Japan. It is at the center of the nation's business, art, and entertainment worlds.

Downtown Tokyo is filled with towering skyscrapers and bustling department stores. At night, bright billboards and signs light up the city.

Tokyo has many beautiful parks and gardens. The Imperial Palace, which boasts many lovely gardens, sits in the middle of the city. Yoyogi Park has a large forested area. Next to Yoyogi Park is the Meiji Shrine, an important Shinto shrine. Ueno Park, in northeastern Tokyo, is full of peaceful walkways and temples. Many of the city's top museums are located within the park. These include the Tokyo National Museum, the National Science Museum, and the Metropolitan Fine Art Gallery.

Tokyo National Museum

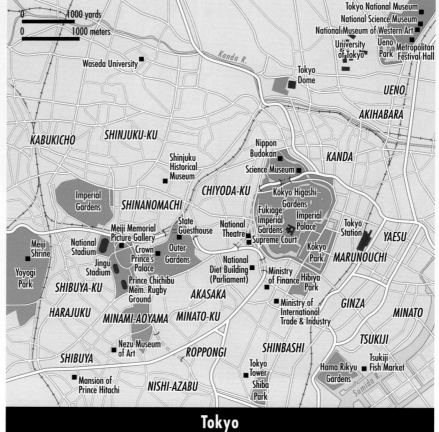

A person must be at least twenty years old to vote in Japan.

Democratic Party of Japan (DPJ) and the Liberal Democratic Party (LDP); two important minor parties, New Komeito and Your Party; and a number of smaller parties. In 2010, The DPJ was in power with 306 representatives and 106 councillors.

The House of Councillors consists of 242 members. A person must be at least thirty years old to run for councillor. Elections for councillors occur every three years, with half

National Government of Japan

Executive Branch

- Prime Minister
- Cabinet
- Ministries

Legislative Branch

- Diet
  - House of Representatives
  - House of Councillors

Judicial Branch

- Supreme Court
- High Courts
- District Courts
- Family Courts
- Summary Courts

of the membership being elected at a time. Of these, 146 councillors are elected from the nation's 47 prefectures, which are similar to states. The Japanese people as a whole elect the remaining 96 from a single national list.

Japan's House of Representatives has 480 members who serve four-year terms. The House of Representatives has greater power than the House of Councillors. New laws must be passed in both houses, but if the House of Representatives votes in favor of a law by two-thirds majority, the House of Councillors cannot stop the law from being passed.

The Executive Branch

Immediately after an election, the first order of business in the Diet is choosing the prime minister. The prime minister is the head of the government and the leader of the cabinet. Japan's prime minister is chosen by the House of Representatives from its members and is usually the head of the political party with the most representatives. Traditionally, the emperor appoints the prime minister, but the emperor is bound by the constitution to appoint the person chosen by the Diet. The cabinet is made up of all the ministers, or department heads. A majority of the ministers must be elected members of the Diet.

The cabinet has specific responsibilities for governing the nation. Japan's cabinet implements laws, signs treaties, and develops a budget that is given to the Diet for approval. The cabinet deals with foreign countries and oversees the general operation of government departments. It chooses the chief justice of the Supreme Court and appoints other judges.

The fifteen members of Japan's supreme court meet in this building in Tokyo.

Sometimes, the leading party does not have a majority of votes in the House of Representatives. Then, the party with the most votes asks representatives from other smaller parties to join them. This is called forming a coalition. When coalitions are formed, parties need to compromise to get things done.

Power among political parties shifts from one election to the next. In order to have a smooth transition from one government to the next, department ministers have shadows. Shadow ministers are leaders from the second most powerful party. A shadow minister in agriculture, for example, would receive all the same information that the minister for agriculture receives. In 2010, the DPJ was in power, but the LDP held a substantial number of seats. If the LDP gains enough seats in the next election, shadow ministers may become actual cabinet ministers in the next government.

Prime Minister Naoto Kan speaks at a meeting of his cabinet.

Prime Minister Naoto Kan

Naoto Kan (1946–) became Japan's prime minister in 2010. As a young man, Kan worked in the patent office. He became interested in politics and won a seat in the House of Representatives as a member of the Socialist Democratic Federation. In 1996, he became minister for health and welfare. After a long career in the legislature, Kan became deputy prime minister in 2009, before becoming prime minister.

The Courts

Japan's court system is based on the U.S. court system. The courts are independent from the other branches of government. The highest court is the Supreme Court, with a chief justice and fourteen justices. The Supreme Court hears cases that have been heard earlier in lower courts. For example, a robbery trial might be heard first in a district court. If the person accused of the crime thinks a mistake was made in the trial, the case may be heard a second time in a high court, and then again in the Supreme Court. The Supreme Court delivers the final judgment on the nation's laws and court rulings.

The Japanese legal system is crowded with cases. In 2009, Japan started a new jury system. Judges in the program are ordinary citizens who work with professional judges. The lay judges hear criminal trials and determine guilt or innocence of the person on trial. The idea is for citizens to become more involved in the process of Japanese justice.

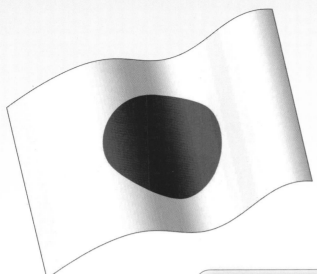

Japan's Flag

Japan's national flag is a white rectangle with a large red circle in the center, which represents the sun. Japan is known as the Land of the Rising Sun. Samurai carried the symbol of the rising sun in the twelfth century during the feud between the Taira and Minamoto clans.

Local Governments

Japan has two levels of local government. The forty-seven prefectures have governors, while mayors govern cities and towns, which are called municipalities. Prefectures have elected assemblies that make laws governing their people. The laws of a prefecture cannot overrule national laws.

The mayor of the small town of Kanna. The Japanese people elect mayors to run towns large and small.

In recent years, many small towns have joined with their neighbors to create new, larger cities. Most towns and small cities rely on the central government for most of their funding. In 1999, Japan had 3,232 municipalities. In 2010, that number had been reduced to 1,727 because so many towns had merged. Municipalities that have five hundred thousand people or more are called cabinet-order designated cities and work the same way as prefectures. They can collect taxes and spend money for their own welfare. There are nineteen such designated cities in Japan.

Tokyo is a busy, sprawling city.

Japan's National Anthem

"Kimigayo" is one of the world's oldest national anthems. The words come from a tanka, a five-line, thirty-one syllable poem, that was written in the tenth century. Hiromori Hayashi, a court musician, wrote the music in 1880. "Kimigayo" became Japan's national anthem in 1888.

Japanese lyrics

Kimi ga yo wa
Chiyo ni yachiyo ni
Sazare ishi no
Iwao to nari te
Koke no musu made.

English lyrics

May my Lord's reign,
Continue for a thousand,
Eight thousand generations
Until pebbles grow into boulders
Covered with moss.

A High-Tech Economy

M IKI IS ABSORBED BY HER CELL PHONE. SHE IS READING a *keitai shousetsu,* a cell phone novel. This unusual literature form was first developed in Japan, where it is incredibly popular among teens. Phone novels are written entirely in text messages. Each chapter consists of seventy to one hundred words. Miki is one of millions of Japanese teens glued to their cell phones. Teen cell phone use has become so overwhelming that most Japanese high schools have banned students from having cell phones in school. As soon as Miki leaves school, she pulls her cell phone from her backpack. She reads the next two chapters of her latest cell phone novel as she waits for the bus home.

The Spirit of Innovation

The Japanese people are into gadgets, innovation, and interesting machines. The Matsushita company is trying to develop an automated kitchen. The owner would return home from work to a hot, well-cooked meal. In other homes, cell phone messages order equipment to water the houseplants.

Opposite: **A worker examines television screens at a factory near Osaka.**

Rooms automatically heat up or lights come on when people enter the home. There are singing mailboxes that musically announce when mail has arrived. Japan even has machines that wash money.

The Economy

About 68 percent of Japanese workers are employed in service industries. These are jobs where one person provides a service for another, rather than making or growing something. Service workers include everyone from computer programmers to bankers, bus drivers to hairdressers. About 28 percent

A service robot demonstrates how it can pick up items.

Dentistry, like all medical work, is a service industry.

of the Japanese people work in industry, making products. The remaining 4 percent work in agriculture. Today, Japan has the third-largest economy in the world. Only the United States and China have larger economies than Japan.

Japan makes products, such as televisions, cell phones, and cars, that are sold throughout the world. Japan's most valuable exports are motor vehicles, semiconductors, electrical machinery,

More than six million cars are built in Japan every year.

and chemicals. Exports are worth more than US$700 billion a year. Japan sells most of its exports to China, the United States, South Korea, and Taiwan.

As part of this international trade, Japan also buys products that its people need. Food is a major import, as are textiles and raw materials. Japan also imports fuel, chemicals, and various types of equipment. Japan's biggest import partners are China, the United States, and Australia. Japan buys food, machinery, and raw materials from these countries. Saudi Arabia and the United Arab Emirates sell Japan oil.

Industry

Japanese companies, such as Matsushita and Panasonic, are known for developing state-of-the-art high-tech products. They have been industry innovators in designing flat screen and high-definition televisions. Throughout the world, people buy Japanese cameras, cell phones, laptop computers, and camcorders. They expect Japanese electronics to be high-quality products.

Japanese factories are modern and productive. Many use robots to build cars, trucks, electronic materials, and plastic goods. Factory workers are well trained and dedicated. In Japan, being a good worker is much admired.

Japan's economy is part of a worldwide economy. Once, an entire car, for example, was made completely in a Japanese factory. Now, car parts may be made in China or South Korea, and, along with Japanese parts, shipped to the United States or somewhere in Europe to be assembled into a car.

Japan also has a number of small- or medium-sized businesses that depend on skilled craftspeople. The Japanese have a love for *monozukuri*,

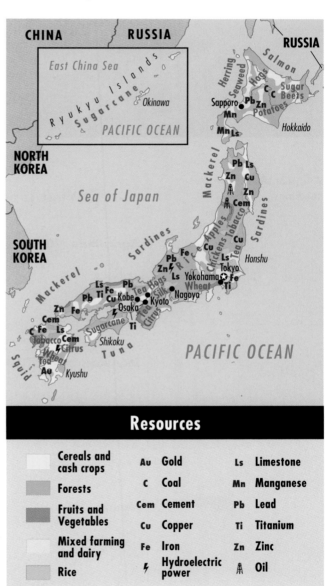

Resources

Cereals and cash crops	Au	Gold	Ls	Limestone		
Forests	C	Coal	Mn	Manganese		
Fruits and Vegetables	Cem	Cement	Pb	Lead		
Mixed farming and dairy	Cu	Copper	Ti	Titanium		
Rice	Fe	Iron	Zn	Zinc		
	⚡	Hydroelectric power	⛏	Oil		

A farmer plants rice seedlings.

What Japan Grows, Makes, and Mines

Agriculture (2010)

Rice	9,740,000 metric tons
Potatoes	2,296,000 metric tons
Sugar beets	700,000 metric tons

Manufacturing (2010)

Cars and trucks	9,625,940 vehicles
Electronic components and devices	US$226 billion worth
Crude steel	109,600,000 metric tons

Mining (2006)

Cement	7,300,000 metric tons
Limestone	1,666,000 metric tons
Titanium sponge	39,000 metric tons

the idea of making things. Small craft shops turn out furniture, textiles, and other handcrafted goods.

Rice: The Staple Food

Japan is smaller than California, and only 11 percent of the land can be farmed. Japan imports about 60 percent of its food.

Rice is Japan's main crop. It is a staple food, one that the Japanese eat every day. Rice grows in paddies, which are fields covered with water. The fields must be used constantly, producing two crops a year. The soil gets worn out and needs large amounts of fertilizer. Japan uses fertilizer more intensively than any other country.

Dry fields, or fields that have to be watered to produce crops, are used to grow vegetables, such as sugar beets, daikon, bok choy, cabbage, cucumbers, onions, and beans. Japanese farmers also produce dairy products and eggs. Livestock is mostly chickens and hogs.

Kobe Beef

Kobe beef is a cut of beef from the black *tajima-ushi* breed of cattle. The cattle are fed beer and are pampered so that their flesh does not become tough. Kobe beef filet mignon steaks are highly prized. One 10-ounce (284 gram) steak imported from Japan costs about US$60.

High tech is not just for manufacturing and factories. Japan uses high tech in agriculture. Rice growing, once done completely by hand, now employs mini-machines that plow and level paddies and plant and harvest rice. Scientists have developed a tomato plant that bears up to ten thousand tomatoes by filtering out the sun's harmful rays. Among other unusual high-tech products are square watermelons and underground rice paddies with artificial lighting. One such rice farm is a former bank vault in the heart of Tokyo.

The Yen

The Japanese currency is the yen, with the symbol ¥. Coins come in 1¥, 5¥, 10¥, 50¥, 100¥, and 500¥. Five yen and 50¥ coins have circular holes in the centers. One yen coins are the smallest, and 500¥ coins are the largest coins.

Paper currency comes in values of 1,000¥, 5,000¥, and 10,000¥. There is also a 2,000¥ bill, but it is very rare. Japanese bills are different sizes and different colors, which makes them easy to tell apart. The 1,000¥ note is basically blue with a portrait of scientist Hideyo Noguchi (1876–1928) on the front and Mount Fuji on the back. The Meiji-era author Ichiyo Higuchi (1872–1896) graces the front of the purple-shaded 5,000¥ bill, with painted irises on the back. The brown 10,000¥ note features Meiji-period educator Yukichi Fukuzawa (1835–1901) on the front and an engraving of a phoenix from Byodo-in Temple on the back. A phoenix is a bird from mythology that dies in a ball of fire and rises from its own ashes. All paper bills have Braille lettering in the lower left-hand corner so that blind people can tell the value of each note.

Fishing and Whaling

Japan's major protein food is fish. Fishing is a major industry in Japan. The country maintains one of the world's largest fishing fleets and takes nearly 15 percent of the global catch. The fish caught includes finfish, such as tuna, and shellfish, such as crabs and shrimp. Japan is also active in aquaculture, or farming fish. Aquaculture provides about 1.5 million tons of fish each year. The most common farmed fish are scallops, Pacific cupped oysters, and Japanese amberjack.

Whaling is a traditional industry in Japan. Conservation groups argue that Japan violates the ban on whaling for food, while Japan claims that whales are caught for research purposes. Whales are caught, and scientists take samples from the whales' bodies. The whale meat is then packaged and sold in supermarkets. In recent years, Japan has taken about four-fifths of all whales caught throughout the world.

Workers unload tuna at a port in Japan. The Japanese eat more tuna than people in any other nation do.

What Does It Cost?

Here are prices for grocery items in Japan.

Item	Price in a Yokohama supermarket	U.S. dollar value
2.2 pounds (1 kg) apples	398¥	$4.77
1 quart (0.95 liters) of milk	230¥	$2.75
¼ pound (113 g) cheddar cheese	500¥	$5.99
½ pound (227 g) pineapple	500¥	$5.99
3 bars soap	200¥	$2.40
¼ pound (113 g) bologna	99¥	$1.18
1 gallon (3.8 L) of gas	375¥	$4.50

Nori seaweed

Harvesting and processing seaweed gives Japan another bounty from the sea. Seaweed is used in soup, such as miso soup, hot pot dishes, and in making sushi. The common seaweed for sushi is nori, which is dried before being sold in sheets.

Mining

Mining is the smallest sector in Japan's economy. Japan's earth does not yield large quantities of iron, aluminum, copper, or coal. Those products are imported to Japan.

Most of Japan's mining activity unearths materials used in industry. These include stone products, such as dolomite, limestone, and silica. The country is the worldwide leader in titanium sponge, making about 28 percent of the world's supply. Titanium sponge is a basic metal product used in making jet engines, missiles, jewelry, and cell phones.

Transportation

Japan's population is always on the go. People travel from city to city on high-speed bullet trains or drive on Japan's many highways in cars, trucks, and buses. Most people use public transportation—buses and commuter trains—since individual cars and the gasoline that fuels them are expensive. Within Japan's nine major cities, subways provide rapid transportation between suburbs and industrial centers.

In addition to being a leading producer of cars and trucks, Japan has an active shipbuilding industry. Huge container ships carrying tons of material move in and out of Japan's busy ports. The country's major ports, such as Nagoya and Yokohama, have ships docking, loading, and unloading around the clock. A network of highways and railroad lines link seaports to internal cities.

Shinkansen

The bullet train—Shinkansen—speeds Japanese travelers from city to city at speeds between 150 and 185 miles per hour (240 and 300 kph). The trains are electric and seat up to a thousand passengers. The most popular service runs between Osaka and Tokyo. Trains depart going in each direction every ten minutes. A central computer in Tokyo controls the movements and speed of the Shinkansen trains.

An Urban Nation

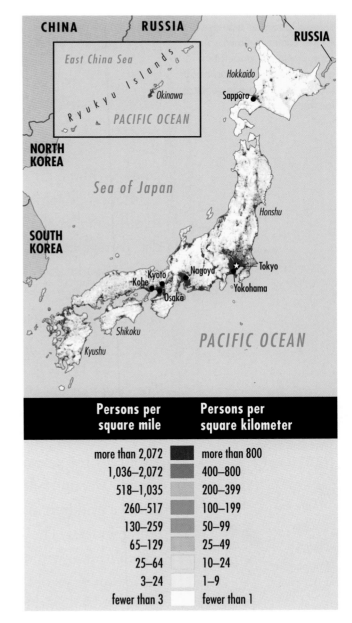

Persons per square mile		Persons per square kilometer
more than 2,072		more than 800
1,036–2,072		400–800
518–1,035		200–399
260–517		100–199
130–259		50–99
65–129		25–49
25–64		10–24
3–24		1–9
fewer than 3		fewer than 1

Nozomi has taken a new job in Tokyo. She is used to living in a city. Her family comes from Sapporo, but Sapporo is not Tokyo. Japan's capital is the center of the world's largest metropolitan area, with a population of more than 35,676,000. Nozomi fights the crowds on the way to and from work, in the shops, and on the subway. At the end of the day, she meets her friends for a night on the town. The problems of crowded Tokyo become the promise of Tokyo as the group heads out to a sushi bar for dinner and a club for dancing and karaoke. There is always something to do in this bustling, international city.

Elderly Japanese exercise at a care center in Nanto. As Japan's elderly population grows, so does the number of facilities that provide services for the elderly.

Population

Japan is home to nearly 127 million people, making it the tenth most populous country in the world. Yet, with a total area slightly smaller than California, the country is pretty crowded. On average across Japan, there are 873 people per square mile (337 per sq km), but many islands have no people at all. Japan's cities, however, are packed with people. In Tokyo, an average of 15,144 people live in every square mile (5,849 per sq km).

Graying Japan

The population of Japan is getting older. In 2010, only 13 percent of Japanese people were under the age of fifteen. Sixty-four percent were fifteen to sixty-four years old. Twenty-three percent were sixty-five years old or older. Young Japanese couples are having fewer children or deciding not to have children at all. At the same time, older Japanese are living longer. The average Japanese man lives to be about seventy-nine, while the average woman can expect to live to eighty-six years old. This is the oldest life expectancy for any people in the world.

Population in major cities (2010 est.)

City	Population
Tokyo	13,010,279
Yokohama	3,654,427
Osaka	2,668,113
Nagoya	2,258,804
Sapporo	1,905,777
Kobe	1,534,000
Kyoto	1,460,000

Because Japan has a very low birthrate, the government faces serious challenges. Japan expects its senior population to be 40 percent of its population by 2050. The aging of the population is called the "1–2–4" problem. This means that families now consist of one child, two parents, and four grandparents. The government provides significant support for the elderly. They get health care, pension money to live on, and even workers to help cook their meals, bathe them, and dress them. These services cost tax money. As fewer children are born, there are fewer taxpayers growing up to support government programs.

Ethnic Mix

Slightly more than 98.5 percent of the population of Japan is ethnically Japanese. Koreans (0.5 percent) and Chinese (0.4 percent) account for just more than 1,000,000 residents, and the approximately 750,000 remaining people are from throughout the world.

There are three native minority groups in Japan. They are the *burakumin*, or *hisabetsu buraku*, which means "discriminated communities"; the Ainu; and the Ryukyuans. The burakumin are ethnically Japanese, but they were traditionally discriminated against in Japanese society. The burakumin have inherited the status of being outcasts. Their ancestors were

A farmer relaxes with his granddaughter in a field.

In traditional Ainu culture, men did not shave.

Ethnic Japan

Japanese	98.5%
Korean	0.5%
Chinese	0.4%
Others	0.6%

butchers, leather tanners, and funeral directors. People who worked in these jobs were outcasts because they went against Buddhist rules against killing and Shinto ideas about handling the dead. About two to four million Japanese are burakumin.

There are fewer than twenty thousand Ainu. This native culture lives in a small area of Hokkaido that was set aside for them by the Japanese government in the late nineteenth century. The Ainu used to speak a different language, but that language is no longer used.

Ryukyuans originated in the Ryukyu Islands, in the southwest of Japan. The culture has strong influences from both Japanese and Chinese heritage. Ryukyuans mainly live on the island of Okinawa.

What's in a Name?

There are over one hundred thousand Japanese family names, but the most common are Suzuki, Sato, and Takahashi. In the same way that many English names come from geographical features—Hill, Stone, and Rivers, for example—Japanese names may also come from the land. Ishikawa means "stone river" in Japanese. Given names also have meanings. Ai means "love or affection," while Masaru means "victory."

The Japanese Language

About 99 percent of Japanese people speak Japanese as their first language. Schoolchildren spend much of their class time learning to read the three written Japanese languages: kanji, katakana, and hiragana. Kanji are the basic characters of the Japanese language. There are thousands of kanji characters, but only about three thousand are commonly used.

Kanji characters originally came from Chinese character forms. Japanese elementary school children are expected to learn 1,006 basic kanji characters. Katakana are modified

A child practices writing Japanese.

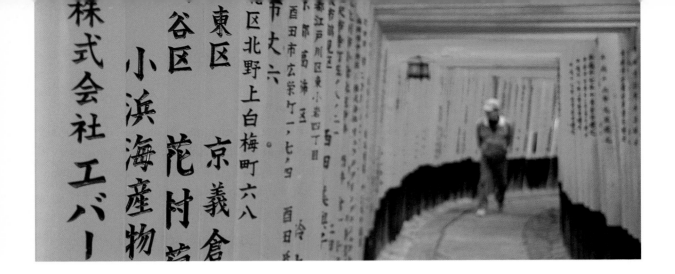

Japanese writing covers the gates at a shrine in Kyoto.

kanji characters used for words or names borrowed from other languages. Hiragana are used to write native words for which there are no kanji, including new words or words rarely seen in kanji. Traditionally, men wrote kanji and katakana, and women wrote hiragana.

Trends in language use are changing. Fifty years ago, all children could read and write kanji. Writing on a computer requires only reading kanji, not writing it, because typing is done on a keyboard. This means people remember how to read kanji, but not always how to write them by hand. In a nationwide exam, fewer than 20 percent of people tested knew the required two thousand basic kanji.

Reading Japanese

The Japanese alphabet has five vowels (a, e, i, o, u) and fourteen consonants (b, d, f, g, h, k, m, n, p, r, s, w, y, and z). Reading Japanese means understanding the vowel sounds of the Japanese language. All vowels are pronounced, and there is no silent "e."

a	"ah" as in *far*
e	"eh" as in *met*
i	"ee" as in *ziti*
o	"oh" as in *solo*
u	"oo" as in *flu*
ae	"ay" as in *day*
ai	"eye" as in *mine*
ei	"eh" as in *let*

Japanese children spend most of their time in school or doing school-related activities. The Japanese school year runs from April through the following March, and many schools hold classes six days a week. By law, Japanese children must attend school from first through ninth grades.

Many schoolchildren wear uniforms. Elementary school boys wear white shirts, short pants, and a ball cap. The girls wear gray skirts and white blouses. On rainy days, children don yellow ball caps and slickers and carry yellow umbrellas. Older girls wear sailor outfits, often navy in winter and white in summer. Junior high and high school boys often have white shirts, ties, and blazers or military-style suits called *gakuran*. These suits may be black, navy, or gray. The jacket has a standing collar and large brass buttons.

Many Japanese school-children wear uniforms.

Children learn music in school.

Children who have turned six years old before April 1 start first grade at the local elementary school. Elementary school usually starts at 8:30 A.M. and goes to 3:00 P.M. Classes are large, often thirty to thirty-five students, with children working in small groups. The subjects taught include the Japanese language, social studies, math, science, and music. Children have physical education regularly, and all schoolchildren must learn how to swim. Because Japanese is difficult to learn, children begin by learning small groups of kanji. Starting in the fifth grade, children also learn English.

Sports Day

Sports Day gives schoolchildren an opportunity to participate in a variety of sports. Sports Day is normally a weeklong event featuring races, ball tossing, and tug-of-war. Classes are divided into teams, and families come to cheer for their children. Sports Day also features bands, traditional Japanese dancing, and cheering contests.

Junior high school covers the same subjects as elementary school. After-school clubs offer sports, such as soccer, baseball, or table tennis. Many students choose to study kendo, Japanese sword fighting, using bamboo swords. Schools have computer labs, and after-school educational computer games entertain many junior high students.

Getting into the right high school makes the difference in determining what college or university students will attend. As a result, many parents arrange for their children to go to *juku*, or cram school, to study for the high school entrance exam.

Japanese high school students take computer classes.

High school is a high-pressure environment with long days. Students sometimes spend twelve hours a day or more in class or studying at home. Math, science, Japanese, English, and history are important, but students who wish to excel also play sports, learn a musical instrument, and study arts and crafts.

Many children go on to junior college, technical school, or university. Junior colleges offer two-year degrees, and nine out of ten students at these schools are women. Students may learn nursing, nutrition, communications skills, or similar subjects. Technical schools offer five-year programs in such topics as computer design and repair, automotive repair, or merchant marine skills. Universities are similar to universities and colleges in the United States.

Temples and Traditions

It is Rin's wedding day. Rin and her family enter the Hokkaido Shinto shrine. She is dressed in a white kimono, called *shiromuku*, a white obi (a sash), and a white headdress. Haruto, Rin's bridegroom, wears *montsuki* (a black formal kimono), a kimono jacket, and *hakama*, which are long, loose gray pants. A Shinto wedding is a private affair. Only the bride's and groom's close family attend.

A Shinto priest offers prayers for the couple for luck, happiness, and the protection of the Shinto gods. Rin and Haruto drink three sips of sake (rice wine) from each of three cups. Haruto reads a marriage agreement, and the bride and groom exchange rings. The families share sake, and the wedding is complete. Family, friends, and neighbors share in the joy of the marriage at the *kekkon hiroen*, a wedding party with a large meal and a wedding cake.

The Way of the Gods

The Japanese people follow Shinto, the way of the gods. It is believed that the gods are all around, and they have the

Opposite: **A Shinto priest leads a wedding party at Meiji Shrine in Tokyo.**

Religion in Japan

Shinto	84%
Buddhism	71%
Christianity	2%
Other religions	8%

The numbers add up to more than 100 percent because many people follow both Shinto and Buddhism.

A Shinto priest prays at a mountain temple. Well over one hundred million Japanese follow some form of Shinto.

power to make people's lives better or worse. Shinto spirits, or *kami*, number in the millions. They are associated with all the natural objects on earth or in the sky. An important god is Amaterasu-omikami, the sun goddess. It was she who took part in the creation of earth and all living things.

Shinto is considered the national faith and is closely connected to the imperial family. It is a religion of the here and now. Two basic elements guide a follower of Shinto. First is purification, which involves washing the hands and the inside of the mouth. The second element is to make offerings to the many gods, or kami. Offerings are followed by prayers, which are usually involved in asking the kami for help or protection. Because the gods are linked to aspects of nature, many rituals happen at the same time as planting and harvest.

Many Japanese have two altars in their homes. One is Shinto and the other Buddhist. Many Japanese people follow both Shinto and Buddhism. Family members will make daily offerings of rice cakes, salt, and holy water to the Shinto shrine. Births and marriages are celebrated in the Shinto way, but funerals follow Buddhist rituals.

A Visit to a Shrine

People enter a Shinto shrine through the *torii*, an archway. The torii is a gateway for believers. Nearby is a purification trough for washing. Just inside the shrine is the offering hall. Believers bring rice cakes or other food items as an offering to the god they pray to. Within the offering hall is a rectangular structure that is covered with *ema*, small wooden plaques. Worshippers write their prayers and desires on the ema and leave them hanging up at the shrine so the gods will receive their wishes.

Shichi-go-san (7-5-3 Festival)

Every November 15, three- and seven-year-old girls and five-year-old boys dress up in their best kimonos. Their families head to their local shrine and pray for the future of their children. The term *shichi-go-san* refers to the Japanese numbers seven, five, and three. Age three is when children are allowed to let their hair grow. At five, boys wear their first *hakama* pants (pleated, skirt-like pants) in public. At age seven, a girl celebrates wearing her first obi (sash on a kimono). Children are not considered fully formed until age seven.

Buddhism

Buddhism came to Japan by way of Korea in the mid-500s CE. By the eighth century, Buddhism had become Japan's national religion. Every town had at least one Buddhist temple, and many monasteries and nunneries were built for people devoted to living the religious life.

Buddhists follow the teachings of Siddhartha Gautama (ca. 563–ca. 483 BCE), who is known as the Buddha. The idea of reincarnation, or rebirth, is important in Buddhism. Through reincarnation, individuals go through many cycles of birth, living, and death, followed by rebirth into a new life. Followers of Buddhism devote their lives to virtue, good conduct, respect for others, prayer, and the pursuit of enlightenment. Wisdom and enlightenment come from a pure, calm mind.

Since the sixth century, many different Buddhist sects have emerged in Japan. Each sect is a school of thought, a group that follows Buddhism in its own way. Today, Japan has more than one hundred different sects. The oldest sects are the Tendai and the Shingon. Other major sects include Jodo, Jodo Shinshu, and Zen.

In 805 CE, a monk named Saicho founded the Tendai sect. The central Tendai temple was built on Mount Hiei, and it is still a center of Buddhist study. Followers of Tendai believe that there is something of the Buddha in all people, so all followers have an opportunity to reach enlightenment. Shingon Buddhism, brought to Japan by Kukai in 806 CE, follows the basic idea that the world reflects the true nature of the Buddha. Followers cannot see the entire world, so their view of life is only a small part of reality.

Buddhist nuns live a simple, focused life filled with meditation and study.

The Great Buddha of Nara is 49 feet (15 m) tall. It was completed in 752 CE.

Jodo, or Pure Land, Buddhism is based on the idea of a person being reborn in the Pure Land or paradise. Introduced by the monk Honen in the twelfth century, Jodo became popular at a time when Japan suffered political problems and corruption. Honen believed that following all the practices of Buddhism was not practical in a time of trouble. He introduced a simpler version of Buddhism based on repeating prayer.

There are many forms of Pure Land Buddhism in Japan, and one of the most popular is Jodo Shinshu. Founded by Honen's student Shinran, Jodo Shinshu made practicing Buddhism easier. Jodo Shinshu priests and monks could marry, which was not allowed in other Buddhist sects. Followers could eat meat, and they did not have to practice many of the more demanding aspects of Buddhism. Jodo Shinshu is now the most common Buddhist sect in Japan.

The word *Zen* means "meditation." Zen Buddhists reach a level of enlightenment or wisdom through meditation, the act of concentrating the mind on a specific topic. The relationship between a follower and a Zen master, or teacher, is basic to Zen Buddhists.

Funerals

Japanese honor their dead for five full weeks. On the day of a Japanese funeral, the body is cremated (burned to ashes). Mourners attend the cremation and eat a small meal there. Afterward, family members of the deceased person pick bones from the ashes. They pass the bones from guest to guest with chopsticks. Following the cremation, a service takes place in a Buddhist temple. Guests give money to the family and receive a small gift in return. The ashes are placed in an urn. The family keeps the urn on an altar in their home for thirty-five days. Incense burns continuously, and visitors come to light an incense stick to honor the dead. At the end of the thirty-five-day mourning period, the urn is buried in a cemetery.

Buddhism dominated Japanese religious practices until the rise of the Meiji emperor. The Meiji government preferred the Shinto religion and named Shinto as the state religion. About ninety million Japanese consider themselves Buddhist. Many

At some shrines, people dress funeral figures in red bibs in the hope that the spirits will clothe the dead in the afterlife.

also follow Shinto beliefs. It is said that Japanese people are born and married following Shinto practices, but they die as Buddhists. Japanese funerals follow Buddhist rites.

Christianity

Other Christians may have traveled to Japan earlier, but the first Christians known to arrive in Japan came in 1549. In that year a Roman Catholic priest, Father Francis Xavier, arrived from Portugal. He convinced many Japanese to become Catholics. The shoguns feared that the growing Catholic Church would encourage European conquest of their country. Christians were treated badly. Many were beaten or killed for their religion. Christians were forced to go into hiding. In the early 1600s, Christianity was banned in Japan.

Seven Gods of Good Luck

The Japanese believe there are seven gods of good luck. Merchants in Kyoto and Osaka in the fifteenth century started the belief that the *shichifukujin* brought good fortune. The gods are Ebisu, Daikokuten, Bishamonten, Benzaiten, Hotei, Fukurokuju, and Jurojin. Only Ebisu was originally Japanese. The others came from China. Ebisu (right) protects sailors at sea. Ebisu's picture was painted on ships before a long voyage to ensure a safe trip. In Kyoto, a vending machine outside a Shinto temple sells charms of people's favorites among the gods. Buy a charm, and enjoy your good luck.

About half a million Japanese are Roman Catholic.

The arrival of Commodore Perry and the U.S. Navy in Japan in 1853 opened the nation to Christian missionaries. In 1873, a law was passed that allowed Christians to practice their religion in Japan. Today, between 1 and 2 percent of Japanese belong to a Christian church. Half a million are Catholics, and another half a million belong to various Protestant faiths. The Orthodox Christian Church and the Jehovah's Witnesses represent the remaining Japanese Christians.

The Arts and More

CHIEKO INVITES HER GRANDPARENTS TO A TEA ceremony, or *sado*. Her apartment is small, so she makes a reservation at a tearoom. The hostess prepares the *matcha*, or green tea. She lays out the bowl and utensils for brewing tea, being careful to place them in an artistic fashion. Tasty food arrives, beautifully arranged on red lacquered trays. Bowing to her grandparents, Chieko greets them. The tearoom hostess offers Chieko's *oji-san* (grandfather) and *oba-san* (grandmother) a small meal, called *cha kaiseki*. The tea ceremony is more than a cup of tea and a bite to eat. It is a tradition of honoring visitors that dates back more than five hundred years.

Music

Classical Japanese music is called *gagaku*, which means "elegant music." Traditional and formal, gagaku is still played at government events. String, wind, and percussion instruments create these classical Japanese sounds. The sound is very different from Western classical music. Japanese music uses a

Opposite: **In Japan, the presentation and drinking of tea is considered an art form.**

The koto has thirteen strings. different musical scale. Common gagaku instruments include the *koto* and *biwa*, which are stringed instruments. A *komo* is a type of flute, and a *shakuhachi* is like an oboe.

Folk music singers perform on the biwa, a type of lute. Long ago, groups of blind and physically challenged musicians traveled Japan, playing for religious events to bring good luck to households. Blind women, known as *goze*, played the koto and accompanied their singing by playing on small lap drums.

Other folk songs, called *min'yo*, represent the music of the common people. The songs may be work songs, religious hymns, songs for weddings or funerals, and children's songs. The annual Obon Festival draws min'yo musicians, playing on banjo-like *shamisen*.

Japanese teens do not listen to gagaku on the radio. Like young people everywhere, they listen to rock, pop, heavy metal, rap, hip-hop, and new age music. Japanese jazz has an active following. Jazz clubs and concerts draw listeners to hear great musicians such as guitarist Koichi Yabori and bop pianist Takashi. Japanese electronic jazz, called nu-jazz, features several internationally known jazz groups, such as Indigo Jam Unit and Quasimode.

A Night at the Theater

Traditional Japanese theater presents three types of plays: Noh, Bunraku, and Kabuki. Noh plays are symbolic dramas, with subjects taken from history or classical literature. Songs,

Kodo

Japanese drum play—*taiko*—hypnotizes audiences. Kodo, one of the most popular taiko groups, combines rhythm, athletics, dance, and entertainment. Drums range from small handheld instruments to huge drums taller than grown men. Kodo adds flute play to the rapid thundering of the drums, creating a visual and sound sensation that thrills worldwide audiences.

Bunraku puppetry dates back to the 1600s.

dances, and stylized movements are done onstage. Noh players wear masks and act onstage with limited props or scenery.

Bunraku is puppet theater. Each puppet is exquisitely made and dressed, and may be a hand puppet or a marionette. Hand puppet theater takes place on a small, enclosed stage. Marionettes may be quite large—3 feet (1 m) or even taller—and are moved by strings. The Japanese also use shadow puppets, which are flat figures that move between a light source and a screen. Bunraku is considered the most highly advanced puppet theater in the world.

Kabuki means "strange or extraordinary," and Kabuki theater lives up to its name. There is nothing realistic about Kabuki. It is fanciful, highly entertaining, and active. The stage has many trapdoors and platforms, and actors rise onto and sink below the stage as the scenes progress. Typical characters in Kabuki include thieves, heroes, samurai, nymphs, and fairies. The themes and costumes are classical, with actors usually appearing in kimonos and traditional Japanese wigs. Makeup is a white face with enhanced lines, wrinkles, lips, and eyes. The different colors of makeup indicate emotions. Red shows happiness, black indicates fear, and pale green represents calmness.

Kabuki actors use rice powder to create the white base of their makeup.

Calligraphy is a respected art in Japan.

One Thousand Cranes

According to Japanese legend, a person who folds one thousand origami cranes will be granted a wish. Sets of colorful origami paper are sold in blocks of one thousand sheets, which allows the artist to spend many happy days folding and stringing together cranes.

Sadako Sasaki

After the end of World War II, a girl named Sadako Sasaki tried to put off her death by folding one thousand origami cranes. Sadako suffered from a type of cancer called leukemia, the result of radiation from the atomic bombing of Hiroshima. Sadako did not get her wish, but her story lives on in books. Today, one thousand origami cranes represents peace.

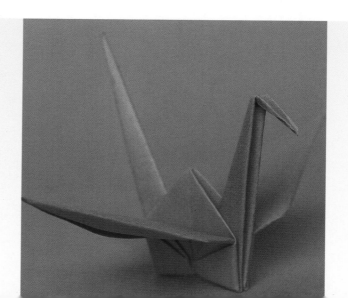

Basho

Basho (1644–1694) is considered Japan's greatest haiku poet. Born Matsuo Kinsaku in Ueno, Basho entered the service of the local lord. Servant and master both loved a form of poetry called *haikai no renga*, which began with the three-line verse we know today as haiku. When the lord died, Basho became a wanderer. He eventually settled in Edo (now Tokyo) and gained fame as a poet. This is one of his poems.

Kareeda ni   On dead branches
karasu no tomari keri   Crows remain perched
aki no kure   At autumn's end

The Japanese have many artistic crafts that are enjoyed by children and adults alike. *Shodo* is beautiful calligraphy drawn with black ink and a brush. *Temari* is a fiber art in which the artist uses multicolored threads to create an elaborate geometric design. Temari is usually used to make children's balls.

Kirie is the art of paper cutting. The artist uses one piece of paper and cuts away bits to leave a silhouette or shadow picture behind. True kirie artists may make hundreds of cuts in a piece to create a scene, often cutting an intricate border to frame their artwork. Other works of kirie employ a small number of cuts, creating a stunning effect with just a few open spaces.

Haiku, Tanka, and Japanese Literature

Japanese literature covers two thousand years of writing. Poetry dates back to the Nara period (710–794) when forty-five hundred poems were published as *Manyoshu, A Collection of Ten Thousand Leaves*. These poems took on many verse styles, but the most popular were the haiku and the tanka.

A haiku is a seventeen-syllable, three-line poem. Common haiku themes include seasons, plants or flowers, and animals. Tanka are thirty-one-syllable, five-line poems covering many of the same subjects as haiku.

As early as 1008 CE, noblewoman Murasaki Shikibu wrote a charming novel called *The Tale of Genji* that is considered the first great work of Japanese literature. It is also thought to be the world's oldest novel. The novel gave readers a peek at what life was like at the Japanese court.

Many women of the time wrote essays and collected folk-tales. Romantic stories of hideous villains and valiant samurai heroes entertained the ladies of the court.

Today, manga stories fill bookstore shelves, but they are not Japan's only modern literature. Since World War II, Japanese writers have produced innovative and thoughtful literature. In 1968, Yasunari Kawabata won the Nobel Prize in Literature

Akira Kurosawa

Tokyo-born Akira Kurosawa (1910–1998) was an award-winning Japanese filmmaker. Kurosawa was best known for *Rashomon*, a murder mystery; *Seven Samurai*, a heroic tale of warriors facing impossible odds; and *Kagemusha*, a historical epic. He directed magnificent battle scenes and made movies that featured flawed characters. Kurosawa said, "I like unformed characters. This may be because, no matter how old I get, I am still unformed myself."

A karate expert blocks a kick.

for his artistic, sensitive writing. In 1994, Kenzaburo Oe also became a Nobel Prize winner. Oe's work deals with political and social issues, such as nuclear weapons and the demands of raising a physically or mentally challenged child. Oe's own son Hikari, a young man with severe brain damage, is depicted as the hero in many of Oe's novels.

Martial Arts

Many Japanese pursue physical fitness through martial arts. There are several different forms of martial arts, from judo and karate to sumo and kendo. The point of judo is to train one's body and become fit. *Judo* means "the gentle way," and skill is more important than strength or power. In karate one uses the fists, elbows, and feet to defend against an attack. *Karate-do* means "the way of the empty hand" because karate does not involve weapons. Fighting in karate is called sparring.

Sumo is a form of wrestling and is Japan's national sport. Sumo wrestlers have large, well-trained bodies. The goal behind a match is to force the opponent off his feet and to the ground. Many matches last only a few seconds or a minute at the most, but that minute can raise a wrestler to the rank of grand champion, the *yokozuna*. Six sumo tournaments take place each year, with matches scheduled daily over two weeks. Japanese people flock to the arenas or around televisions to watch their favorites compete.

Kendo, the art of the sword, is Japanese fencing. The idea originated with the samurai, who were experts with both long and short swords. Junior high students join kendo clubs and train with bamboo swords. Experts wear long black pants and wire-mesh masks but fight barefoot. A fencer scores from the number of hits and his or her aggressiveness toward the opponent. As with other martial arts, kendo requires physical and mental training to succeed.

Competitive Sports

Competitive sports begin in local schools. Children join school teams or learn sports in physical education classes. Some join sports clubs after school or train for careers in sports with private coaches. In the little free time children have, many like to join Little League baseball or play on soccer teams. Figure skating has become popular since Mao Asada and Shizuka Arakawa became world champions.

Japan's corporations play an active role in local and regional sports. They sponsor youth teams in baseball, soccer, rugby,

Japan's Most Popular Athlete

In 2010, Japanese baseball fans voted Ichiro Suzuki (1973–) their favorite athlete. Called simply Ichiro, he is the greatest baseball player to come out of Japan. He went straight from high school to the Japanese major league team the Blue Wave. In 2001, Ichiro left Japanese baseball behind and signed with the Seattle Mariners. By 2010, he had been named to the All-Star team ten times and won ten Gold Glove Awards for his work in the outfield.

volleyball, basketball, and table tennis. At the adult level, workers play for the honor of their companies. Basketball and baseball seem to attract top players, who may earn more than US$200,000 a year to work part-time jobs and play for their corporations. Once, more than two hundred corporate teams played in organized leagues. Today, economic problems have forced many companies to give up their corporate teams.

A young girl competes in the Japanese table tennis junior championships in Tokyo.

The Arts and More **113**

Japanese soccer players celebrate a goal during the 2010 World Cup.

Baseball is one of Japan's most popular sports. From Little League through major league teams, baseball brings parents and fans out to the ballpark. Japan has twelve professional baseball teams. Several Japanese players have left Japan to play for American baseball teams. Japanese fans are loyal and continue to follow their heroes wherever they play.

Girls and women play fast-pitch softball, and, like the men, a professional league attracts top athletes. At the 2008 Olympics, Japan stunned the United States team and won the gold medal in softball.

Japan has a professional soccer league, the J-League. In 2002, the FIFA World Cup was jointly hosted by Japan and South Korea. This drew a large number of Japanese fans to soccer fields and encouraged young athletes to play soccer. In 2010, Japan's national team enjoyed great success at the World Cup in South Africa. They made it to the round of sixteen, which is the farthest a Japanese team has advanced in men's soccer. Japan's women's national team has been among the top ten teams in the world since 2008. The women play in the Women's World Cup and are always among the top teams playing.

Just for Fun

Japanese children spend much of their free time outside. Japanese people are avid bike riders. Tokyo has a bike path, which is used by children heading to school and workers hurrying to their jobs.

Many Japanese are enthusiastic gardeners, although their gardens are small. For many years, Japanese have pursued the fine art of bonsai. This is a long-range gardening skill used to grow dwarf, perfectly shaped trees. Japanese prefer evergreens for bonsai because their beauty lasts throughout the year.

Let's Go Fight a Kite

Yes, kite fighting attracts huge crowds. The Takogassen, a kite-fighting festival held in Shirone, has a three-hundred-year-old tradition of battling demons and fierce dragons. More than three hundred people fly kites that weigh as much as 110 pounds (50 kg). Teams of thirty to fifty men pull their kites toward each other. The kites dart and dive against their opponents. The first to cut through the other's line wins.

Living in Japan

IT IS THE SECOND MONDAY IN JANUARY, AND IT IS KAZUO'S Coming of Age Day. In Japan, young adults celebrate turning twenty on Seijin no Hi, Coming of Age Day. At age twenty, young Japanese are considered adults. Coming of Age Day is a national holiday. Kazuo's parents have planned a big party, and Kazuo will receive many gifts to honor this important day. Because this is a family celebration, Kazuo gets his hair cut and buys a new suit. He'd rather wear jeans and sneakers, but Kazuo knows how important this day is to his parents and grandparents.

In the Home

Japanese homes are quite small. Yards, for those who have them, are also small, and homeowners often refer to their yards as "fitting on a cat's forehead." Limited space has spurred Japanese creativity. They grow miniature trees and plants that yield vegetable crops. They have compact cars, televisions as thin as a candy bar, and beds that fold up and can be tucked out of the way during the day.

Opposite: **Japanese young people dress up to celebrate on Coming of Age Day.**

A boy serves himself rice from a steamer.

Kitchens are tiny, so appliances are sometimes smaller than they are in the United States. Some Japanese refrigerators, for example, tuck under countertops. Many Japanese people shop for food almost daily. The major purchase is large quantities of rice. Most families have an electric rice steamer that is set at night and turns out freshly made rice for breakfast. Many kitchens have heated tables, where the family eats during the winter. Clothes are washed in a small washing machine in the kitchen and hung on the balcony or patio to dry.

Television

When people do have time off, many families watch television. Japan has more televisions per household than the United States. Japanese people watch news and documentaries. Reality shows are also popular. One popular show features people sitting around a library table. A contestant gets a card with instructions to do a bizarre activity, while the others try not to laugh. Another show has contestants running over an obstacle course—and usually ending up in muddy water. A popular cooking program shows ordinary cooks producing dishes using ingredients that are not labeled. The end result is not always edible, but it is interesting.

In Japan, mothers are typically responsible for taking care of the children.

The Family

Family members have specific roles in the family's life. Traditionally, fathers are responsible for earning money. They may spend the week away from the family, sleeping and eating near their workplace and traveling home only for the weekend. In most cases, mothers are responsible for paying bills, managing family money, keeping the home, shopping, and raising the children. Mothers supervise the children's education, which consumes plenty of time.

Japanese children do not have chores. What they do have is school, studies, school activities, and schoolwork. If that sounds like a lot of school, it is. Even elementary school children spend most of their time involved with learning.

The thin ends of chopsticks that hold food rest on a holder, not on the table.

At the Table

Rice is the staple food and is served at every Japanese meal. In Japan, a family meal is one course with several side dishes. Diners drink soup from a cup and eat the rest of their meals with chopsticks. The rice is sticky so it is easy to eat with chopsticks. During a meal, if the chopsticks are not being used, they are set on a chopstick rest—never on the table.

A Picnic Lunch

Throughout Japan, both the old and young look forward to lunch, when they have a *bento* box to tuck into. Bento boxes are common carriers for school lunch, workers' lunches, picnics, and even take-out foods. Bento is a two-section lunch box loaded with goodies. On one side is rice. No Japanese meal would be complete without rice—either sticky white rice or flavorful fried rice. The other compartment has an array of foods that go with the rice: vegetables, fruits, cooked egg, grilled fish, sushi, fried pork, sausage, or tuna. Bento boxes offer quality, healthy foods.

Favorite Japanese Foods

daifuku	a rice cake stuffed with fruit filling for dessert
donburi	a bowl of rice with chicken and egg, pork and egg, beef, or seafood
gyoza	dumplings filled with meat and/or vegetables
nori	seaweed used in sushi dishes or as a topping for rice dishes
ramen	noodle soup
soba	buckwheat noodles used in place of rice, like thick spaghetti
sushi	raw, picked fish and rice dishes, often made with seaweed
tempura	battered, deep-fried fish, meat, or vegetables
tofu	soybean curd
yakitori	grilled, skewered chicken

A traditional Japanese breakfast includes rice, and side dishes might be grilled salted salmon, salty pickles, pickled soybeans, an omelet, and miso soup. This breakfast is a lot of work to produce before family members head off to work or school. Many families settle for toast or sausages and eggs.

Japanese lunch is a boxed lunch, called *bento*. Both children and workers take bento with them for lunch, and they are popular on picnics or when traveling. For convenience, people can buy prepackaged bento in shops, train stations, and supermarkets.

Dinner is much like lunch, with rice as the central dish and a selection of side dishes. At times, Japanese replace the rice with soba, a type of noodle. Noodle soup is common, and many people stop in noodle shops to pick up a dish for lunch or dinner.

Japanese have fast-food shops, including their share of hamburger, fried chicken, and pizza places. True Japanese fast-food stores sell noodles, rice with some type of topping, or

People in Japan wear jeans, skirts, and suits, just like people in North America do.

street foods that are sold in booths. Noodle shops sell ramen (noodle soup), soba (like spaghetti with meat or vegetable toppings), or udon (noodles in broth). Rice plates may be hot or cold and have toppings such as pork and egg, beef and onions, or fried shrimp. Quick foods are sold from carts or in convenience stores. They can be pancakes wrapped around pork or vegetables, grilled chicken on skewers, or cups of stew.

What to Wear

Most Japanese people wear Western-style clothing, which may be jeans and T-shirts, suits, dresses, or casual gear. Sports are popular, so most people also have jogging suits, shorts, and sneakers. However, for work and special occasions, most Japanese have specific outfits. Some jobs require a uniform, and special occasions need traditional Japanese garb.

Many Japanese people, both schoolchildren and workers, wear uniforms. Employees may travel to and from work in a suit and change into the company uniform when they get to work. For some jobs, a *hopi*, or cotton jacket, with the company logo is the accepted uniform.

Traditional Japanese clothing for men is a dark kimono. The word *kimono* simply means "thing to wear." The outfit is made up of hakama, which are loose-fitting, wide-legged pants, and a *haori*, a short coat. Made from silk, traditional male kimonos can be quite expensive. A top-of-the-line kimono and pants can cost as much as US$10,000.

A young boy dresses in traditional clothes for a festival.

Many kimonos feature flower designs.

A classic ladies' kimono is a T-shaped, straight robe. It is loose fitting, with long sleeves and flowing skirts. The kimono is held in place by a sash, called an obi. Footwear is usually *zori*, which are thong-style sandals. Women's kimonos come in a silken rainbow of colors, and the best kimonos have embroidery. A spring kimono might be pale yellow or pink, with a pattern of butterflies and cherry blossoms. An autumn kimono would be a darker color and feature autumn maple leaves. A woman's kimono may cost far in excess of US$10,000, depending on the material and the embroidery. A single obi can cost half as much, and the total outfit—kimono, obi, ties, socks, sandals, hair accessories, and fans—can easily run up to US$20,000.

Celebrating Together

The New Year begins with the tolling of Buddhist temple bells. The bells ring 108 times at midnight. During the day, people eat noodles as a symbol of long life. They visit a Shinto shrine, then stop in to see friends or family.

One of Japan's most delightful holidays is Children's Day. Held May 5, this is a day when parents honor children by flying carp-shaped kites or banners. The day is part of Golden Week, which also includes Greenery Day and Constitution Memorial Day. Workers get paid time off, and there are festivities all week. For many families, Golden Week is the only joint vacation they have all year.

National Holidays

January 1	New Year's Day
Second Monday in January	Coming of Age Day
February 11	National Foundation Day
March 20	Spring Equinox
April 29	Greenery Day
May 3	Constitution Memorial Day
May 5	Children's Day
July 20	Marine Day
September 15	Respect for the Aged Day
September 22	Autumnal Equinox
October 14	Sports Day
November 3	Culture Day
November 23	Labor Thanksgiving
December 23	Emperor's Birthday

At the end of Obon, people release lanterns to guide the spirits of their ancestors back to where they came from.

The Obon Festival is not a legal holiday, but it is important to Buddhists. Usually held during July or August, the Obon Festival is a time to honor one's ancestors, care for family graves, and pray for one's family. Buddhists believe that the spirits of loved ones return to visit during Obon. During the Obon Festival, there is music, dancing, and food.

Japanese follow both the regular, or Gregorian, calendar and a lunar calendar. They believe in lucky days and look at their calendars to find a lucky day for a wedding or other important event. Sundays in November, for example, are lucky days to get married.

There are also lucky and unlucky years. The Japanese use the Chinese zodiac system, which names each year for one of twelve animals. The years follow a twelve-year cycle. In Japan, 2011 is the year of the hare, while 2012 is the year of the dragon, and 2013 is the year of the snake. The year of the hare is lucky for getting married or having children. However, children born in the year of the dragon can be a handful. They are believed to be ambitious, powerful, and daring.

The Japanese culture is an active mix of the new and modern, the ancient and traditional. Throughout Japan's cities, skyscrapers rise beside Buddhist temples that are hundreds of years old. Japanese people embrace modern technology and creativity. They also honor the customs and beliefs of their ancestors. There are few countries that balance new and old as skillfully as Japan.

About two thousand Buddhist temples and Shinto shrines are sprinkled throughout Kyoto, a city of 1.5 million people.

Timeline

Japan History

Humans arrive in Japan from Asia.	33,000–30,000 BCE
People develop fishing skills and begin to grow rice.	8000–300 BCE
The first bronze tools appear, and people establish permanent farming villages.	ca. 300 BCE
Shinto becomes the official religion in Japan.	ca. 0
Japan begins using the Chinese alphabet.	500 CE
Manyoshu, A Collection of Ten Thousand Leaves is the first Japanese collection of poetry published.	ca. 759
The samurai rise to power.	1050
Famine kills hundreds of thousands of Japanese.	1181
Kublai Khan tries to invade Japan.	1274
Christianity is made illegal.	ca. 1630
The emperor bans foreigners from Japan.	1641
Mount Fuji erupts.	1707
The United States forces Japan to allow trade with foreigners.	1854

World History

ca. 2500 BCE	Egyptians build the pyramids and the Sphinx in Giza.
ca. 563 BCE	The Buddha is born in India.
313 CE	The Roman emperor Constantine legalizes Christianity.
610	The Prophet Muhammad begins preaching a new religion called Islam.
1054	The Eastern (Orthodox) and Western (Roman Catholic) Churches break apart.
1095	The Crusades begin.
1215	King John seals the Magna Carta.
1300s	The Renaissance begins in Italy.
1347	The plague sweeps through Europe.
1453	Ottoman Turks capture Constantinople, conquering the Byzantine Empire.
1492	Columbus arrives in North America.
1500s	Reformers break away from the Catholic Church, and Protestantism is born.
1776	The U.S. Declaration of Independence is signed.
1789	The French Revolution begins.

Japan History

The yen becomes the new currency.	1871
The first railway line connects Tokyo and Yokohama.	1872
The Satsuma Rebellion ends with the samurai defeated.	1877
Japan holds the first democratic elections outside of Western nations.	1879
Japan defeats China in war and takes Taiwan as a colony.	1895
Japan defeats Russia in a war and takes control of Korea.	1905
Japan sides with the Allies in World War I.	1914
An earthquake destroys much of Tokyo.	1923
All Japanese men gain the right to vote.	1925
Japan invades Manchuria, the northeastern part of China.	1931
Japan goes to war against China.	1937
Japan bombs Pearl Harbor, Hawaii, and the United States enters World War II.	1941
The United States drops atomic bombs on Hiroshima and Nagasaki; Japan surrenders.	1945
Japan's current constitution is written.	1947
Japan becomes the second-largest economy in the world.	1964
Toyota introduces the Corolla, the best-selling car of all time.	1966
Japan's economic bubble bursts, and the stock market falls.	1991
One hundred forty-one nations adopt the Kyoto Protocol to reduce greenhouse emissions.	2005
A magnitude 9.0 earthquake sets off a tsunami; about 25,000 people are killed.	2011

World History

1865	The American Civil War ends.
1879	The first practical lightbulb is invented.
1914	World War I begins.
1917	The Bolshevik Revolution brings communism to Russia.
1929	A worldwide economic depression begins.
1939	World War II begins.
1945	World War II ends.
1957	The Vietnam War begins.
1969	Humans land on the Moon.
1975	The Vietnam War ends.
1989	The Berlin Wall is torn down as communism crumbles in Eastern Europe.
1991	The Soviet Union breaks into separate states.
2001	Terrorists attack the World Trade Center in New York City and the Pentagon in Washington, D.C.
2004	A tsunami in the Indian Ocean destroys coastlines in Africa, India, and Southeast Asia.
2008	The United States elects its first African American president.

Fast Facts

Official name: Nippon or Nihon (Japan)

Capital: Tokyo

Official language: Japanese

Tokyo

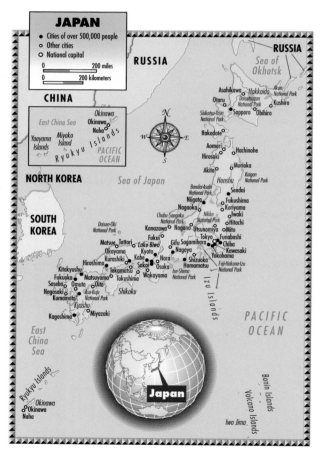

Japan's flag

Mount Fuji

Religion: No official state religion

National anthem: "Kimigayo," adopted in 1999, music by Hiromori Hayashi

Government: Parliamentary government with a constitutional monarchy

Chief of state: Emperor

Head of government: Prime minister

Constitution: May 3, 1947

Area: 145,882 square miles (377,833 sq km)

Highest elevation: Mount Fuji, 12,388 feet (3,776 m) above sea level

Lowest elevation: Hachiro-gata, 13 feet (4 m) below sea level

Longest river: Shinano River, 228 miles (367 km)

Largest lake: Lake Biwa, 259 square miles (670 sq km)

Largest island: Honshu, 810 miles (1,300 km) long; 140 miles (230 km) wide

Total number of islands: 6,852

Length of coastline: 18,486 miles (29,750 km)

Average annual precipitation: 61.5 inches (156 cm)

Lowest recorded temperature: –42°F (–41°C) in Asahikawa, on January 25, 1902

Highest recorded temperature: 105.6°F (40.9°C) in Tajimi, Gifu, on August 16, 2007

Nagoya Castle

National population (2010 est.):		126,804,433
Population of major cities (2010 est.):	Tokyo	13,010,279
	Yokohama	3,654,427
	Osaka	2,668,113
	Nagoya	2,258,804
	Sapporo	1,905,777

Population density: 873 per square mile (337 per sq km)

Population distribution: 66% urban; 34% rural

Famous landmarks:
- ▶ *Imperial Palace,* Tokyo
- ▶ *Nagoya Castle,* Nagoya
- ▶ *National Museum,* Tokyo
- ▶ *Mount Fuji,* Central Honshu
- ▶ *Shitenno-ji,* Osaka

Economy: Japan has the world's third-largest economy. It is among the world's largest and most advanced producers of cars, electronic equipment, machine tools, steel, ships, chemicals, textiles, and processed foods. Major crops grown in Japan include rice, sugar beets, and potatoes.

Currency: The yen. In 2011, 83.44¥ = US$1.

System of weights and measures: Metric system

Literacy rate: 99%

Currency

Schoolchildren

Common Japanese words and phrases:

ohayougozaimasu	Good morning
konnichi wa	Good afternoon
sayonara	Good-bye
ogenki desu ka	How are you?
genki desu	I'm fine
hai	Yes
iie	No
sumimasen	Excuse me
doumo arigatou	Thank you

Ichiro Suzuki

Prominent Japanese:

Emperor Hirohito (1901–1989)
Emperor during World War II

Yasunari Kawabata (1899–1972)
Nobel Prize–winning author

Akira Kurosawa (1910–1998)
Academy Award–winning filmmaker

Kenzaburo Oe (1935–)
Nobel Prize–winning author

Murasaki Shikibu (ca. 978–ca. 1026)
Author of the world's first novel

Ichiro Suzuki (1973–)
Baseball player

Osamu Tezuka (1928–1989)
Father of manga art

To Find Out More

Books

▶ Greene, Meg. *The Technology of Ancient Japan*. New York: Rosen Publishing, 2006.

▶ Hardyman, Robyn. *Japan*. New York: Chelsea House, 2009.

▶ Kalman, Bobbie. *Japan: The Culture*. St. Catharines, Ontario: Crabtree Publishing Company, 2008.

▶ Levin, Judith. *Japanese Mythology*. New York: Rosen Central, 2007.

▶ Mofford, Juliet Haines. *Recipe and Craft Guide to Japan*. Hockessin, DE: Mitchell Lane Publishing, 2010.

▶ Phillips, Charles. *Japan*. Washington, DC: National Geographic Press, 2009.

▶ Richardson, Hazel. *Life in Ancient Japan*. St. Catharines, Ontario: Crabtree Publishing Company, 2005.

▶ Spencer, Linda. *The War at Home: Japan During World War II*. San Diego, CA: Lucent Publishing, 2007.

▶ Turnbull, Stephen, and James Field. *Real Ninja: Over 20 True Stories of Japan's Secret Assassins*. Brooklyn, NY: Enchanted Lion Books, 2008.

Music

▶ Ensemble Nipponia. *Traditional Vocal and Instrumental Music (Japan)*. Nonesuch, 1990.

▶ Iwamoto, Yoshikazu. *Traditional Japanese Music*. Continuum, 1994.

▶ Saeki, Satomi. *Japanese Traditional Koto and Shakuhachi Music*. Oliver Sudden Productions, Inc., 2005.

▶ *…Very Best of Japanese Music*. Arc Music, 2005.

Web Sites

▶ **CIA Factbook: Japan**
https://www.cia.gov/library
/publications/the-world-factbook
/geos/ja.html
For information about the people, government, economy, communication, and history of Japan.

▶ **Japan National Tourism Organization**
www.jnto.go.jp/eng/
This site is sponsored by the Japanese government and provides extensive information for people traveling to Japan.

▶ **Kids Web Japan**
web-japan.org/kidsweb
Check out this Web site for fun content that will help you learn more about Japan and the customs of the Japanese people.

Embassies

▶ **Embassy of Japan**
2520 Massachusetts Avenue NW
Washington, DC 20008
202/238-6700
www.us.emb-japan.go.jp/english
/html/index.html

▶ **Embassy of Japan in Canada**
255 Sussex Drive
Ottawa, ON K1N 9E6
Canada
613/241-8541
www.ca.emb-japan.go.jp

Index

Page numbers in *italics* indicate illustrations.

Meet the Author

BARBARA SOMERVILL HAS BEEN A WRITER FOR MANY YEARS. She loves learning about new places, cultures, and cuisines. Learning about Japan for this book was fascinating. One thing that always interests her is how people live their daily lives. Somervill could not go directly to Japan to find out this information, but she did get to visit via YouTube. Many Japanese and foreign visitors post films of grocery shopping, their apartments, going to school, Sports Day, and traveling on the Shinkansen. Someday, Somervill hopes to visit Japan, but, in the meantime, YouTube, books, and DVDs provide armchair travel experience.

Photo Credits